To the g... ...
lady E. ...
mins Amtns.'
—Finley Lin .

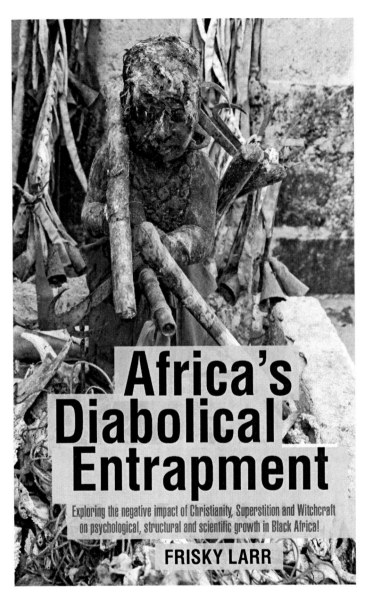

Africa's Diabolical Entrapment

Exploring the negative impact of Christianity, Superstition and Witchcraft on psychological, structural and scientific growth in Black Africa!

FRISKY LARR

authorHOUSE®

AuthorHouse™
1663 Liberty Drive
Bloomington, IN 47403
www.authorhouse.com
Phone: 1-800-839-8640

Edited by Engr. Sunny Irumekhai, M.Sc. P.Eng

Published by AuthorHouse 1/28/2013

ISBN: 978-1-4817-8285-2 (sc)
ISBN: 978-1-4817-8296-8 (e)

Table of Contents

Dedicated to Prof. Bola Akinterinwa

(Director-General, Nigerian Institute of International Affairs)

Preface

When I heard an African Pastor saying six years ago, that Africa is now more spiritually advanced and developed than the rest of the world, I couldn't help but hold my breath. I asked myself how dumb it could all be! I had no doubt that we were not oblivious to the plight of the African continent in all aspects of life that I do not need to recount in this work.

Spiritual advancement means nothing else than enduring pains and sufferings on earth in absolute submission to worship and faith in the hope of reaping affluence in the life beyond – in God's paradise! Many societies have long gone beyond this point while elements within the African fold now attempt to put a spin to the reality of being left behind.

Unfortunately, they find a fertile ground amongst folks riddled with poverty and adverse economic conditions.

Then come witch doctors spreading fright and awe to every nook and cranny of Sub-Saharan Africa. Folks have accepted the notion through several generations and ages that witches, wizards and spirits of departed souls play a huge role in their daily lives. Today, the African society is virtually split in two with the range of the gray zone hardly identifiable. One part seeks solace with witch doctors and shrines and worship God the way their ancestors did thus rendering credence to the unproven base of the belief in witchcraft. The overwhelming majority of the other part commits to Christianity not the way the rest of the world knows it but in a peculiar manner that makes Pastors mini-gods with the oracular powers of seeing visions and being the medium between the congregation and God.

Unfortunately however, the Pastors do not wait to reap their affluence in heaven – in God's paradise! They are enriched and live in affluence with the little drops of sweat trickling down the pockets of their poor peasant followers. The total sum of collections made regularly, now see African pastors counting amongst the multi-millionaires of this world. Yet they are not short of support from the exploited poor. I compare this weird state of mind with the *Stockholm Syndrome* known in hostage taking. It just can't be true!

I therefore seek to present my point of view in this pseudo-scientific analysis to serve as an eye-opener to those who care to get the message.

My name is Friday Agbonlahor (pen-named "Frisky Larr"). I dedicate "Africa's Diabolical Entrapment" to Professor Bola Akinterinwa (Director-General of the Nigerian Institute of International Affairs) for his insistence on seeing my real name spelt in print. All my private reasons notwithstanding, Prof. Akinterinwa will settle for nothing. He is unable to understand that I do not make my country of origin proud by telling the world my African name while Nigerians today are almost exclusively associated with fraud and crime across the international sphere.

I sincerely hope that he and other readers of "Africa's Diabolical Entrapment" will understand my imperfect efforts in this contribution and jump aboard the bandwagon of seeking to polish Africa's intellectual integrity by spreading the message of academic wisdom.

Introduction

The picture of Africa in the mind of Non-Africans has hardly changed over centuries. It has remained constant since the discovery of the continent for colonial adventures. While this cannot be attributed to the stagnation of values in the continent alone, the extent of real change for the better in Africa (in spite of abundant resources) has always remained a controversial issue tearing experts apart. Also through several centuries! One fact though, has always remained constant: Underdevelopment.

Africa has consistently held the conspicuous banner of last among equals on every race to measure development and affluence. It has been associated with all forms of negative impacts ranging from hunger, civil wars, poverty, wild life and everything that primitivity represents. Growth and development have thus been hindered in the continent by all the negative elements.

While corruption and failure of governments have played a major role in the obvious stagnation and actual backward development in the continent, the reason for a glaring lack of awareness among the folks has been a huge mystery. After all western education is not restrained in the continent.

The pseudo-scientific analysis undertaken in *Africa's Diabolical Entrapment* seeks to unravel this mystery by probing deeply into the role played by religion and widespread traditional beliefs in witchcraft, spirits and gods. It seeks to dispel a growing trend amongst a section of Black Africans that is fostering a sense of denial of negative attributes while promoting the positive sides of African values. At the same time, it challenges the new school of thought amongst indigenous leaders of the Christian faith claiming that Africa has now overtaken and is thus more advanced than leading world powers in *spiritual development* (whatever that means).

Africa's Diabolical Entrapment undertakes a comparative analysis of global geographical regions with a journey through the history of beliefs exposing Africa's instrumental exaggeration of imported values. It catalogs a number of dreary events representing the vanity of beliefs in witchcraft and spiritual powers. It identifies the failure of governments in ignoring a trend of mass stupefaction to the benefit of inefficiency at the top. After all, mass awareness is a potent and lethal weapon for demanding public accountability which may translate into a huge albatross with the potential to drown any government anywhere in the world.

Africa's Diabolical Entrapment concludes with projections for Africa for the next two to three decades and recommends measures for curbing the menacing impact of beliefs in witchcraft, spirits and gods on the psyche of the folks! The catalog of real-life events exemplifying elements of retrogressive contents in Christian and traditional beliefs may prove to be breathtaking and simply thought-provoking!

Chapter 1

The Concept of Witchcraft and Sorcery As Seen in the Western World!

I remember lessons in primary education. We were taught to learn a name by heart. The name was Mary Slessor. This Scottish lady, so we were taught in history classes, was a missionary who lived in Nigeria working to gain converts into the Christian religion. She experienced firsthand, a weird traditional practice in the city of Calabar. Calabar is one of many vibrant Nigerian cities in the riverine delta region south of the country which also served as a seaport and the administrative capital of the colonial government of the then British protectorate.

For reasons of belief in the misfortune visited on families and communities by the birth of twins, Calabar nurtured an age-old tradition. A tradition of killing twins at infancy whenever they were born alive while the mothers were left to suffer their pains in the stigma of carrying misfortunes in a fateful pregnancy! Calabar was home to a traditional regime of some grief and horrendous acts.

It is the grief of being the random victim of nature to suffer this fate of nine futile months of pregnancy. The grief of losing the product of joyous expectancy! There was no ultrasound scan in those early days of the twentieth century, at least in Nigeria. Conceived sexes could not be ascertained at pre-natal stages. Pregnant women lived in fears and the gambles of their lives, not knowing what would come out of a pregnancy. I can feel almost in my own depth, how fervently they may have prayed that nature should not bestow on them, the curse of bearing twins in pregnancy.

Mary Slessor lived among the Efiks and the Okoyong – prominent ethnic groups in the city of Calabar. She could not accept the traditional practice of killing twins and worked assiduously to have the practice abolished. One way or the other, she succeeded. The killing of twins was stopped in Calabar and it all happened way before January 13, 1915 when Mary Slessor died.[1]

No one knows what hurdles she faced in those early days of the last century. We do know however, that communities all over the world hardly take kindly to disregard and disdain for traditional values and fight very fiercely to preserve them the way they have been passed over through generations before them. This is especially so when such disrespect to social values and tradition are shown by strangers to their host communities. I will make bold to characterize this notion as a timeless axiom. Mary Slessor succeeded. But I have no doubt that her success may not have come without varying degrees of domestic resistance by the natives.

In retrospect however, it will be easy to assume in our current world of the 21st century that those days are long gone with their peculiar dynamics and more primitive settings of educational retardation.

Unfortunately however, the reality of practicing this archaic belief even to this day (early years of the 21st century), has hardly changed. The village of Ikpe Ikot Nkon is home to the riverine folks of Ibibio. It was here on October 08, 2011 that the 95-year old Ukpong Uyong was murdered in cold blood at the village square of his ancestral home. He was accused of being a wizard.[2]

The notoriety of the community of Ikpe Ikot Nkon does not derive solely from being home to the strange happenings of the "debasement" of children accused of wizardry. Ikpe Ikot Nkon is also privy to the administration of lynch justice in the aftermath of such charges. Children, very much like adults get ostracized, maimed and lynched after being accused of sorcery.

AFTERMATH OF LYNCH JUSTICE:
BADLY BURNT HANDS OF A WITCHCRAFT SUSPECT

This is by no means, an isolated case of rural community life in African societies. The difference from big city life in the practice of beliefs and traditional values derives largely from the crude impunity of administering jungle justice on the abstract charges of sorcery and base witchcraft, which is largely enhanced by the dominant natural setting of rural life with less modern educational impact on general mindset.

Unfortunately however, the belief in sorcery or witchcraft is not limited to the black African continent or any single nation of the world. It is an age-old phenomenon that mankind has lived with from the beginning of time. It is an element of man's endeavor to seek answers to the great unknown and the mystery of being.

In Nigeria as in several other African countries, there is the widespread belief that the phrase "Witchcraft" and "Wizardry" represents the gender-based differentiation of one and the same act. It is believed for instance that the word "witch" is used when the sorcerer is female and wizard used when the sorcerer is male. Many do not know that this is not necessarily true. While the word witchcraft in the English language is generally associated with the feminine gender and not commonly used in describing males engaged in sorcery, the word "wizard" is by no means confined to the male sorcerer. In fact, a wizard may not even have to be a sorcerer. While magical powers in legends and fairy tales are attributes of wizardry, the English language even often uses the word "wizard" these days as a term of positive recognition of excellence in the appraisal of skills in any field of activity. A computer wizard or a wizard at mathematics will simply be describing excellence and skills in the fields that the word is associated with.

While the three words (witchcraft, sorcery and wizardry) all share the common attributes of supernatural powers and the invocation of spirits, the term wizard is clearly the mildest of them all. The invocation of evil powers and harmful magic are readily associated with witchcraft and sorcery and a witch is oftentimes used also to describe an ugly old woman and rarely but sometimes too, qualifies "a charming or alluring girl or woman".[3]

In the history of mankind's development through the ages of Spiritism and primitive beliefs, there are hardly disputations of any sort that the natural phenomenon of rain, thunder and lightning, which the science of physics has today successfully simplified as a precipitation-related process were, in the early days of mankind regarded in awe and worshipped metaphysically. Today, the online encyclopedia "Wikipedia" has this simple scientific explanation as to how rain and thunderstorms occur: *"As the warm, moist air moves upward, it cools, condenses, and forms cumulonimbus clouds that can reach heights of over 20 km. As the rising air reaches its dew point, water droplets and ice form and begin falling the long distance through the clouds towards the Earth's surface. As the droplets fall, they collide with other droplets and become larger. The falling droplets create a downdraft of air that spreads out at the Earth's surface and causes strong winds associated with thunderstorms."*[4]

Some centuries ago however, mankind sang a different tune. The lightning across the sky and the colorfulness of the rainbow all had their unique and pervasive metaphysical significance. Traditional societies that are still focused today, on the worshipping of the rainbow and thunder phenomenon can be safely assumed to have significantly reduced in numerical strength.

The ocean waves have had different meanings of religious connotation to different societies at different points in time and still do for some. Thunderstorms could mean the fury of the gods while lightning may mean an impending divine anger in the realms of wild speculations. Rain itself may have represented different meanings in the facets of human imagination at different points in time. Many phenomena today are routinely accepted as unspectacular in the broad spectrum of natural occurrences thanks to the advancement of scientific understanding and explanations.

This has inadvertently created a state of affairs in which the attachment to and stronger beliefs in lesser scientific phenomena of life's experiences are deemed to characterize lesser developed and more primitive societies.

The undisputable reality that science till today is yet unable to explain the origin of life beyond all reasonable doubts has fanned the flame of the continued search for a credible explanation.

This search for a credible explanation has prompted several conflicting and varying theories and hypotheses in our present day. In fact, one basic reason that the two major religions of the world (Christianity and Islam) have survived the test of time lies in the inability of science to provide a conclusive explanation of the origin of life. The more difficult this process proves to be, the easier it will always be with all attendant impacts, for mankind to embrace the notion of an underlying irrational and non-scientific explanation of the existence of a supreme and omnipotent deity! One ultimate force that requires just faith and belief rather than logical explanations! The concept of God!

For this reason, it matters very little today what scientists like Professor Stephen Hawking have to say on the concept of being as long as science has no foolproof explanation of the creation of life.

Prof. Stephen Hawking is one splendid specimen of human nature and an exceptional intellectual personality with the gift of being a genius. This Englishman was born in Oxford in the year 1942. At the tender age of 21, he was diagnosed with a motor neuron disease known as Amyotrophic Lateral Sclerosis (ALS) – a paralysis-related disease that saw him lose his ability to move in gradual progression. After diagnosing him with ALS, doctors had expected him to die within two to three years. The loss of mobility in his arms and legs in the gradual progression of the disease was followed by the loss of his voice in 2009. This followed from the complicated treatment of some pneumonia infection that led to an emergency surgery to salvage what was left of his ability to speak. This exceptional wheelchair Professor now speaks with the aid of a voice synthesizer – a computer device that makes it possible to get comprehensible words out of his near motionless body. He has been living with this illness since over four decades. "A Miracle of sort" some would say.[5]

Today, from the confines of his wheelchair with the aid of his voice synthesizer, he is an academic celebrity in the capacity of a Theoretical Physicist and a Cosmologist. He has authored several scientific books (leaving several observers wondering how this feat is achieved) and made several public appearances in academic presentations. According to the online encyclopedia Wikipedia, he is an honorary Fellow of the Royal Society of Arts and a lifetime member of the Pontifical Academy of Sciences and holds the highest civilian award in the United States since 2009 - The Presidential Medal of Freedom.

For many religious adherents, this is the stuff that piety is made of. This is a man who many will regard as representing the wonders of God and the need for the total submission to God's infinite mercy. Unfortunately for religious adherents, the Lucasian Professor of Mathematics who taught at the University of Cambridge for 30 years with all attendant handicaps till the year 2009 is a scientist to the core. He is however, obviously, not at all disposed to sharing the emotional views of God's infinite mercy on the weak and the handicapped. He does not seem to believe one bit in religion and the notion of life after death.

In fact, Prof. Hawking only stops short of saying that there is no God at all. *"A belief that heaven or an afterlife awaits us is a "fairy story" for people afraid of death"* he was quoted as saying in a recent interview with the Guardian.[6]

The views represented by Professor Hawking underscores the crucial divide between religion and science.

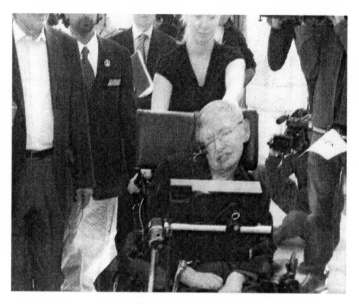

PROF. HAWKING

"I have lived with the prospect of an early death for the last 49 years. I'm not afraid of death, but I'm in no hurry to die. I have so much I want to do first,"

„I regard the brain as a computer which will stop working when its components fail. There is no heaven or afterlife for broken down computers; that is a fairy story for people afraid of the dark "[7]

As contained in the Guardian, he was explicit in his book "The Grand Design" on the claim that "there is no need for a Creator to explain the existence of the universe." The "Big Bang", which till date has been widely acclaimed scientifically as the point of commencement of the universe as it is known today, has always left questions unanswered. Science has nurtured the assumption that *"all of the matter and energy of space was contained at one point"* from which *"a tremendous explosion started the expansion of the universe"* about 15 billion years ago. That is the theory of the Big Bang![8] Questions had to be answered as to the being and creation of this "one point" with specific reference to the catalyst of the "tremendous explosion". Prof. Stephen Hawking advances the notion that this occurrence may not necessarily be the creation of any God. He points to some inevitability of the explosion at this singular point of the Big Bang as a consequence of the law of gravity. He therefore posits that one does not require a Creator to explain how the universe was formed. The controversy greeting this claim comes largely in the aftermath of reactions from the religious community. It underscores this ever-crucial dispute along the way in the search for the origin of life.

This quest for a credible explanation is the underlying groundwork of all forms of religious and metaphysical orientation. It is the mother of all human beliefs in the natural and supernatural worlds. One of such beliefs is of course, the phenomenon of witchcraft, wizardry and sorcery.

The Halloween Phenomenon

Students and adherents of English Literature will easily recall references to witches and sorcerers in William Shakespeare's play Macbeth – written in the 16th or 17th century. The descriptive images often portray old, haggard looking women dressed in long flowing gowns, sometimes with a Chef's apron posing before a mighty broth with long spoons preparing magical potions in a cauldron. Such women usually have long noses and wear a long conical hat with a tiny tip.

CARTOON IMAGES OF HALLOWEEN WITCHES

This is the most typical of several possible descriptions of a witch that any average European will provide in any casual non-scientific conversation. Children's bedtime storybooks casually paint pictures of this sort as do fairy tales and legendaries. They provide images of a dark dreary feminine creature flying through the air sitting on the long grip of a broomstick. In fact, as one website puts it *"Witchcraft is hard to describe in general. There are many forms to suite ones needs or what one wants to believe. There is no central authority or doctrine. No holy book to refer to. There are many different traditions and rituals. Which god dictates ones opinion and style or gods are worshiped."*[9]

A formal investigation into the concept of witchcraft and sorcery in Europe quickly uncovers a vast domain of public ignorance and scanty information. People just do not know what to tell an inquisitive African what or who precisely a witch is or what she looks like, save the recollection of images from fairy tales and legendaries. In most cases, an inquisitive African may end up teaching the European all that he/she needs to know about witchcraft, from the reservoir of ready African knowledge. It is latest at this juncture that the fact becomes clearer that witchcraft and sorcery as a concept in Europe and the western world at large, is very much a relic of history. Almost everything that is known in this field in our present day is drawn from historical records and efforts to keep history alive.

A more careful observation however uncovers another strange reality. A reality that points to a huge regional gap between societies in Europe! The more deprived and economically less buoyant societies of southern Europe housing more ancient and mystical traditional values **seem** to offer a stronger tendency toward superstition and supernatural beliefs than are the richer societies of northern and western Europe. Emphasis is placed here on "seem" to underscore the speculative and non-scientific nature of the assumption.

The story of a blood-sucking Count Dracula from Transylvania (part of present-day Romania) is as fictional and unscientific as human imagination can go. Today, it however, still does not fail to thrill some citizens of Romania and countries beyond, who are proud to identify with the phenomenon. An anonymous reader once remarked on an Internet forum: *"I heard somewhere that to the Romanians, Dracula is viewed the same way that Americans view Abraham Lincoln, and to call Dracula a blood sucking tyrant would be like calling Honest Abe a mad man as well"*.[10]

Many countries in the Balkan (Countries of Southern Europe stretching from Albania, through Bosnia/Herzegovina and Bulgaria to Turkey and Yugoslavia) are home to a huge population of itinerant and nature-loving Gypsies. At the time of writing this book, "Journeyman Pictures" a British video documentary group was running an Internet footage on Youtube titled "Romanian Witches" profiling a self-proclaimed 'white witch'. It features a Romanian Gypsy lady who claims to be a witch with powers to reach out and fight evil forces. The Gypsy population is by all means one of the most traditional races of Europe. Largely concentrated in the Balkan region, the Gypsies can be found virtually in every nook and corner of the globe. They are no strangers to the concept of witchcraft. Orthodox Greece and Russia much like Roman Catholic Italy are all no strangers to the concept of the devil, evil forces and Spiritism.

In western and more northerly European Countries such as Finland, France, Germany, Great Britain, the Netherlands, Norway etc., economic conditions and the overall level of affluence much like the quality of public education, are generally considered pacesetting. Great Britain, Germany and France are not regarded as the economic powerhouses of Europe for the fun of it. It is basically in these societies that the idea and concept of witchcraft and superstition seems less pervasive than it is in the southern counterpart. Indeed, the more traditional segments of these societies – mostly immigrant and indigenized immigrant communities – spearhead the presence of such beliefs. Else, the only traces of the concept of witchcraft in Western Europe can be dug out of historical realities looking back at the days of the Inquisition in early centuries and traditional records of growth and social development.

One such prominent reality of history is the Halloween tradition. Halloween today is celebrated on the 31st of October every passing year. It is a day in which people mark a historical occasion, which origin is hardly remembered by anyone. Today, the night between October 31st and November 01st is usually marked with a virtual costuming party. Discotheques and private parties are flooded with weirdly dressed individuals feigning what memories are left of the physical looks of witches and wizards. Pumpkins are cut to different shapes to symbolize some weirdness of sort.

For those who take this event seriously though, the Halloween presently plays the role of a century-old vehicle for the transmission of oral history. For a vast majority of present-day celebrants however, the Halloween is nothing else but a simple party day like any other that is enjoyed on New Year's Eve or Valentine day. One fact is however certain: It is the fact that Halloween keeps memories of things alive that were once read about and learnt only in history! Facts that cannot be taken for granted. It seems to give a face to the weirdness of facts that have always stayed abstract and beyond independent imagination.

Records suspect that the Halloween may be traced back to an old Celtic tradition. A tradition that was lived centuries ago in the region covered today, by Ireland, the United Kingdom and Northern France. The Celts lived in this area 2000 years ago. Halloween was timed to be celebrated on the borderline *"between fall and winter, plenty and paucity, life and death"*.[11] It was a time for celebration and superstition. Records uncover that there was an ancient Celtic festival called "Samhain" in which people lit bonfires and wore costumes "to ward off roaming ghosts".

Way back in the eighth century, Pope Gregory III was reported to have ordained November 01st as a public holiday in honor of Saints and Martyrs.[12] In fact, the word "Hallow" is an old English word for a Saint or a holy person. It also stands for consecration (making holy) and reverence. The hallowed (holy) turf of Wimbledon readily comes to mind in this respect.[13] November 01st was the "All Hallows" (All Saints) day and also marked the New Year day of the Celts. All Hallows eve is today's Halloween celebrated in the night of October 31st.

Today, save for costumes and the somber, spooky fun tradition thrilling kids and adults alike, Halloween is more about partying than witchcraft and superstition. An online history site reports thus:

"On the night of October 31 they celebrated Samhain, when it was believed that the ghosts of the dead returned to earth. In addition to causing trouble and damaging crops, Celts thought that the presence of the other worldly spirits made it easier for the Druids, or Celtic priests, to make predictions about the future. For a people entirely dependent on the volatile natural world, these prophecies were an important source of comfort and direction during the long, dark winter."[14]

Precisely this dependence on the "volatile natural world" is the pervasive element that this Celtic society of 2000 years ago seems to have in common with the physical state of rural African communities and the mental state of a huge section of urban African elites in our present day. But this will be treated in further detail as this discourse progresses.

Indeed, the Halloween experience in Europe ignites memories of the self-imposed Roman Catholic battle against heresy in the 12th century under the banner of "Inquisition". Weirdness and political dissent were equated with witchcraft and critical books were burnt in public as the inspired work of evil minds.

The Canon Law was the basis of exorcism and the supremacy of Catholicism.

It rekindles memories of the historical witch-hunt of 17th century colonial Massachusetts as recounted by Arthur Miller in his play "The Crucible". This was America's own version of primordial times and the domineering influence of man's basic instincts.

The evolution from these primordial days to our present level of civilization shows how far mankind has come. Superstition and the belief in natural phenomena and the great 'Unknown' is obviously an inherent element of human nature probably from the humble beginning of times. It seems like the base point of consciousness from which social evolution commenced in human communities and psyche. Today, man has come a long way on the journey to civilization and technological advancement for public welfare.

The Shared Values of Symbols in Superstition

In spite of all these advancements though, there are common values that tie mankind to one another no matter the geographical point of origin. Beliefs and values have gone through varying cycles of evolution depending on the geographical location. Superstition however remains one common property shared by mankind in spite of variation in intensity.

There is and has always being another variation too. The variation in forms! This is always a matter of symbols.

Today in Europe, *"Hocus-pocus, Filibus and Abracadabra"* are kindergarten incantations with which children re-echo fantasies of yesteryears that they hardly know anything about. Children feigning the mastery of magical tricks and playing the invocation of some supernatural powers chant these words in pastime games.

The Romanian witch mentioned above and featured in a YouTube footage[15] exemplifies the typical status of the practice of witchcraft in Europe today in the 21st century. She is reported to be the daughter of one late "Mother Caterpillar" who served the deceased wife of former Romanian President (Nicolai Causcescu) as a fortune teller. Her incantations go ways beyond "Abracadabra". She maintains a shrine littered with symbols of different sorts. It has the replica of a human skull, an owl, candles of different colors, a crucifix and a bowl of water containing several flower-leaves and several Tarot cards that she reads for fortune telling. This self-proclaimed witch is an orthodox Christian. She calls herself a 'white witch' devoted to the good of mankind fighting evil forces. She relates from the most significant night of the year shared by Romania's self-proclaimed witches – the "Midsummer Night". A night, in which Romanian witches prepare to witness the opening of the sky and the direct convergence of heaven and earth! She talks of rituals and several weird powers of clairvoyance. She does nothing but fortune-telling and has the following of some urban population, who come for serious consultations to live by her predictions. One of her Clients "Diana" characterizes Jesus Christ as none else but a simple magician.

This footage of Mother Caterpillar's daughter clearly illustrates the contradictory status of the concept of witchcraft in Europe today. The combination of the Christian faith with extra-sensory perceptions and the advancement of supernatural powers is the cornerstone of the semi-religious practice.

A German Researcher Bernd Harder, of the Society for the Scientific Investigation of Parasciences (Gesellschaft zur wissenschaftlichen Untersuchung von Parawissenschaften [GWUP]) warns that superstition is very much alive also in Western Europe. *"One doesn't have to go to Romania or Russia to experience exorcism. Every day, there is about half a dozen exorcists here in Germany, who operate in a semi-legal manner on the fringes of the big churches."* He believes that Bishops are even aware of this even though they often prefer to ignore the phenomenon.
(16)

Remarks left by viewers of the footage of the Romanian witch on YouTube however, clearly reflect the level of acceptance accorded this movement and perception in modern day Europe. The Southern part of Europe with a relatively higher level of acceptance of this practice stands out in clear distinction from the north. Reactions in the forms of comments left on the YouTube page range from ridiculing, denials and outright condemnation of the self-proclaimed 'white witch'. Some Romanian commentators even insist that the lady should rather be referred to as a Gypsy than Romanian. Indeed, the belief in and practice of witchcraft as understood in European civilization is very much drawn along the line of the presentation in this footage across several Southern European countries. Charms, amulets and talisman of various sorts are attendant elements of the practice of this supernatural belief.

The more affluent and richer societies of Northern and Western Europe however, seem to thrive less in this social state of mental conviction. This is not to say however, that these societies do not have their own shares of superstition and symbolic associations.

Oral tradition throughout Europe and many other parts of the world relates for instance, that Friday the 13th is a day in which the most misfortune befalls mankind. This superstition holds the date to be a day of pre-ordained "bad luck". The Germans regard the day Friday as the unfortunate day of the crucifixion of Jesus Christ and the number 13 as an unlucky number. This pathological fear of Friday the 13th called "Paraskevidekatriaphobia" (a Greek compound word) can be so awful that some extremely superstitious Europeans will choose to call off important appointments on this date for fear of reaping unlucky results. Some even fear getting up from their bed. Unfounded claims suggest that the most traffic accidents happen on Friday the

13th. In fact, the German Automobile Club ADAC investigated this claim in the year 2009 and disproved it with a purely scientific result showing that a total of 894 road accidents were reported on a Friday the 13th as opposed to 975 on any other random date. [17]

The black cat is another serious symbol of misfortune across several countries of the European continent. The sight of a black cat across the road upon leaving home for any private or business mission is often construed as a very bad omen for the outcome of such missions. This is true of Germany; it is true of Russia and it is true of several other European countries. It is also of vital importance to observe from which side of the road the black cat emerges. Emergence from the left often symbolizes exacerbated misfortune.

The more catholic societies like Poland for instance, regard wedlock on Christmas day as the greatest heralding of a happy marriage ever after. The month of marriage must bear a name containing the letter "R" in Polish language if misfortune is to be averted and altogether, there are six months with the letter "R". Many Poles believe that a marriage may pay a heavy price if the groom sees the bride in the wedding gown before the day of wedlock[18]. For some unexplained reasons, oral tradition advises women against haircut during pregnancy to avoid trimming off the intelligence of the unborn baby. A red ribbon attached to the bed of a new born baby is generally seen as shielding the child from voluntary and involuntary evil wishes. While moving into a new home, the Poles will traditionally bring the photo of the Holy Mary as the very first object into the new home. This is followed by tables and chairs. Bringing a bed as the first object into a new home may cause an early death in the household while the picture of the Holy Mary guaranties fortune.[19]

Three out of every five Pole (59%) for instance, believe strongly that there are people with the ability of clairvoyance or second sight. This was released in a study by the Polish Center for the Study of Public Opinion (Centrum Badan Opini Spolecznej [CBOS]).

In a representative sampling of public opinion, 48% of respondents were found to believe that there are truly people who are capable of foretelling the future while 39% believes in telepathy and the existence of another intelligent civilization somewhere in the universe. A strong 34% of representatively interviewed respondents believe in the possibility of evil powers afflicting humans.[20]

Germany

One of every two Germans (51%) believes in superstition according to a representative polling of public opinion in the year 2005. While women are most superstitious (62%) only 38% of men admit superstitious tendencies. The most widespread object of superstition in Germany as uncovered by the study is the belief in the four-leaf clover as a good luck charm. This belief is shared by 40% of respondents.

THE FOUR-LEAF CLOVER OF THE CLOVER PLANT

Almost one in every four German believes in the positive force of the number 7. Fifteen percent of respondents believe in the negative prophetic power of any accidental breakage of a mirror. It signals an impending misfortune. Getting up from bed in the morning and stepping out of bed with the left foot before the right is always viewed with suspicion in Western Europe. Every subsequent mishap throughout the fateful day is always jokingly attributed to stepping out of bed on the left foot.[21]

There is indeed, an endless list of superstitious belief in symbols and events through civil societies in Europe often dictated by the degree of piety and conscious metaphysical orientation amongst the folks. This hypothetical distinction can be observed for instance in social tendencies obtainable in the orthodox societies of Greece and Russia as well as the Roman Catholic societies of Italy and Poland as opposed to the less conspicuously religion-dominated German, Dutch, Danish, Norwegian or Swedish societies.

Aside from being widely condemned by the more popular religious community, superstitious behavior poses the scientific challenge of investigating the correlation between the general level of education and belief in and practice of witchcraft. A German survey published on December 12th 2005 uncovers that the higher up the educational ladder people climb, the less confidence they have in superstitious beliefs. While 78% of Germans with elementary education and without any vocational qualification were found to have stronger trust in the veracity of superstitious beliefs, only 40% shared the same view amongst high school and university graduates.[22]

The North-South divide in Europe is even more pronounced by the infiltration of superstition in political life. There are persistent stories of Politicians – particularly in Southern Europe – who are said to consult fortunetellers or horoscopes to aid their decisions on important political issues. There were even complaints that the presidential electoral campaign of Romania in the year 2009 was decided by black magic. The German news portal "Deutsche Welle World" reported the complaint of some consultants of the losing candidate Mircea Geoana claiming that the eventual winner of the race Traian Basescu had afflicted their candidate with a curse. The curse of the "violet flame"! Basescu had worn a violet necktie on the final TV debate. Some of his supporters wore violet shirts or pullovers.[23]

Explaining the background, the Deutsche Welle Romania Expert Robert Schwartz reported that a

Romanian Esoteric introduced the "violet flame" as a form of meditation to the Romanian society. His coming out to explain that it is impossible to use the violet flame as a curse against political opponents did not quell the controversy. Some Social Democrats were convinced after losing the presidential election that parapsychology was definitely at play.

The philosopher Michael Schmidt Salomon working for the Giodarno Bruno Foundation puts it in a nutshell: *"Technologically we are living in the 21st century but our philosophy of life is to a large extent, still shaped by millenniums-old myths and legendaries."* To him, superstitious imaginations are not just harmless whims. They can constitute a serious threat to the health and life of unsuspecting people. The fundamentalist belief in the ability to exorcise evil spirits or cause the disappearance of lethal cancer tumors with a hand-touch often deny the victims the opportunity of useful medical interventions at the right time.[24]

Bernd Hadder puts it more bluntly that there are cases in which *"some irredeemably crazy exorcists killed their victims either through violent actions or because they deny useful medical treatment."*[25]

Today, Russia is planning to introduce legislation to protect victims of superstitious rituals from the grips of Charlatanism because official estimation puts annual death figures in the hands of Miracle Healers at about 500.[26]

Altogether it can be seen that the concept and practice of superstition and witchcraft in the western world is very much an issue on the fringes of social consciousness following phases of metamorphosis through the ages. Even though with varying regional intensity dictated by cultural and traditional orientations, it is safe to admit that an overwhelming aspect of social life in Europe and the western world is very much dictated by rational and scientifically verifiable realities. Compared with exemplary traditional societies in the Caribbean Islands (Haiti, Cuba) and in South America (Brazil etc.) as well as several societies in Africa, Europe and the western world is hardly riddled with shrines, occultic priests, animal sacrifices and a day-to-day life controlled by the superstitious interpretation of routine occurrences. Occurrences that ordinarily and scientifically, would have been seen in mundane awareness! Animism, witchcraft and the practice of fetishism today, is largely lived in the movie screens in the dramatic re-enactment of long-gone historical realities. Movies like "Harry Porter" and the "Lord of the Rings" are the most notable examples.

This civilization nonetheless also has organized practices of reliving the life of supernatural ideals as transferred from previous generations in a historical reinstatement of long forgotten lifestyles. The movement of Satanism today is a metamorphosing replica of the diabolical consciousness of centuries long gone.

Youth Movements in the Example of Satanism

The deep-rooted influence of oral history transported through the downward chain of advancing generations seems to inform the existence of the cult of Satanism in the modern-day western world. The online free encyclopedia Wikipedia describes Satanism as *"a group of religions that is composed of a diverse number of ideological and philosophical beliefs and social phenomena."* What all these religious movements seem to have in common is their reverence or "veneration" for the character of Satan and in some cases, rejection of the Christian faith. Today, this seems to have transformed into reverence for rebellion in general and daring characters in particular – reminiscent of the daring Prometheus of ancient Greek mythology. History reports of Prometheus as a demigod in ancient Greece, who stole fire from the gods and gave it to the human race. Prometheus is thus regarded as a defiantly original creature standing up against the evils of the establishment.[27]

Satanism is often represented by the downward pointing pentagram or the inverted cross.

THE DOWNWARD POINTING PENTAGRAM   THE INVERTED CROSS

Today, the numerically highly decimated movement includes the "Theistic Satanists", "The Luciferianists", "The Palladists" and the relatively more exposed LaVeyan Satanism, etc.

Aside occasional headline-catching rituals amongst high school youngsters organized in one mischievous cult group or the other, not much is heard of Satanism in media headlines today. This most publicly exposed version of Satanism today, is what experts and observers call the *"Pseudo or Adolescent Satanism"*. The often, deadly and blood-spilling rituals associated with this movement (whenever they make headline news) are handled in the category of crime and homicide investigations. Wikipedia reports that this *"liminal experience, reserved primarily for shock value ... does not necessarily imply actual interest, or even belief, in the rites, symbolism, and philosophies of the various forms of Satanist religious practice"*. The symbols are even used in Black Metal Music to induce weirdness and awesomeness. Developments in the present-day western world have shown that

Satanism in public perception hardly goes beyond mischief-making by youngsters in orgies of drinking and fun-induced altercations.

In its ritualistic exercises and exposure to public consciousness in our present-day, the cult of Satanism amongst youngsters can be roughly equated to cultism in Nigerian Institutions of higher learning without the wide followership and criminal elements in thuggery and robberies prevalent amongst Nigerian cultists. There is hardly much left today in the western world, of what Satanism used to be in the early centuries of calendar reckoning.

Away from the youths and the pastime manifestation of fun-time Satanism however, the more serious and better organized models like the LaVeyan Satanism (founded in 1966 by the late Californian lady Anton Szandor LaVey) and its likes, function very much like mainstream religious movements. In addition to the Church of Satan, there is also the Satanic Bible (written by LaVey). While attacks against these movements by the larger religious movements of Christianity and Islam with stronger numerical followership equate the movement with witchcraft and ungodly activities, records however show that the activities of the movements are largely based on rational and cognitive philosophy. *"Its teachings are based on individualism, self-indulgence, and "eye for an eye" morality"* reports Wikipedia on the LaVeyan Satanism. Ironically, the LaVeyan Satanism is reported to be a protagonist of atheism. Satan is regarded *"as a symbol of man's inherent nature."* [28]

A Brief Look at Latin America and the Far East

In fact, an appraisal of superstition, diabolism and animism in the world – no matter how brief and flimsy – will be incomplete without a mention of the practice of this phenomenon in Latin America and the Far East.

The practice of supernatural rituals and beliefs in the American continent is by all indications, more widespread in the southern region of the continent and parts of the Caribbean Islands. From the Brazilian Santeria to the Haitian Voodoo, the practice of animism reigns supreme amongst the peasant and immigrant Black African communities housing erstwhile plantation laborers transported to the region from Africa as slaves of past historical days. Indigenous Red Indian communities also practice their peculiar version of animism. Aside the Island of Haiti with a predominantly peasant black population and by implication, nationwide practice of voodoo, other countries in the region such as Brazil basically run two-class societies in which the practice of animism shows a distinctive social divide. There is a high suspicion – in the absence of vital statistics – that the level of education plays a role in the depth of involvement in the practice of extra-scientific animist or fetish activities across the South American region.

Using Brazil as a typical example I set out to hold informal conversations with as many Brazilians as I could come across. This non-scientific but fact-finding interaction clearly uncovered one reality. The reality that the practice of animism in Brazil cuts across the races and educational strata even though the level of education, social status and even racial belongingness may reflect differing levels and intensities of involvement! Everyone I spoke with is highly convinced that almost every Brazilian has had one direct or indirect interaction or the other within the realms of animist and fetish rituals.

The peculiar nature of South American Societies is the hybrid blend of religious branding reflecting three cultural and traditional backgrounds. The indigenous population of Red Indians no doubt had and still has its own brand of animism with peculiar and unique explanations of unknown natural phenomena. The slaves from the West Coast of Africa dominated by the Yorubas are credited with the introduction of multiple deities in their own explanations of unknown natural phenomena. The European Colonialists from Portugal and Spain stand out as the Ambassadors of Catholicism. Religious trends in South America are therefore a mixture of these three different backgrounds with the black immigrants reportedly blending into closer alliance with the indigenous Indian folks in the aftermath of ostracization. Colonial powers reportedly outlawed animism and other forms of paganism. The ensuing secret practice of the accustomed traditional religions of the immigrant African slaves and the indigenous

Indians was said to have created a state of practical religious solidarity. The resultant product is a religious hybrid.

In our example Brazil, the society is inundated by three known religious trends called Umbanda, Quimbanda and Candomble. The practice of these religions is largely manifest in the propagation of clairvoyance, perception of the spirit world and alternative medicine.

Indeed, every Brazilian I spoke with had a perception of witchcraft that is much similar to the widespread perception in the western world of Europe and North America. A witch is usually the haggard looking old woman with a long nose and the power of clairvoyance, evil practices and the ability to fly. At least in the pre-historic perception! Today however, many Brazilians seem to agree that the definition of a witch is a relative affair. A witch could be anyone with the power of clairvoyance. The power to perceive beyond the limits of our five senses!

Umbanda is therefore characterized as the practice of white magic featuring several gods (Shango, Ogun, Omoli, etc.) and Spirits (Pure and good spirits of the Christian world like the Virgin Mary, spirits of the dead – peculiar to the old black slaves etc.). Umbanda has indeed migrated from Brazil to other South American countries such as Argentina and Uruguay. Umbanda rejects witchcraft and blood spilling as in animal sacrifices and encourages singing, dancing and the divine usage of cowry shells etc. as a method of transporting religious benefits to needy followers.

Quimbanda is the direct opposite of Umbanda. It is the black magic of old black slaves in the nearest form to originality as passed from generation to generation. It includes all forms of witchcraft, evil perception, etc. It subscribes to the viability of multiple gods, rituals, sacrifices, etc.. This is the sole religious mode with the least penetration of catholic values.

Candomble is widely seen as a mixture of both religions.

Each religion reportedly runs publicly approved centers for confronting all social, spiritual and health problems of the individual free-of-charge. Centers that may as well be viewed as clinics in which imaginary or "spiritual" surgeries may be performed! Peasant folks unable to seek medical care for any ailment often resort to the herbal and spiritual combination of an Umbanda Priest while the vengeance-seeking self-perceived victim of injustice may seek the intervention of the Quimbanda Priest to confront his enemies with the power of Ogun (god of war). The Candomble Priest, who may combine both adopts the instrument determined by him/her to be adequate and suited to the troubles of the client.

In any case, even if pretended and indeed light-years away from target, the South American overall view of animism and fetishism is subjected to a subtle drift if not edging towards the world of scientific implementation.

In sharp contrast to this and as will become obvious as this discourse advances, the Caribbean Island of Haiti presents a picture that differs distinctively from any of these trends and shows a clear proximity to the practice of paganism in Africa in hardcore Voodooism. The Quimbanda voodoo practice is widely perceived to be in full force in Haiti with all intensities that equate it in the least, with the status of the practice in Black Africa.

Aside acupuncture and several other herbal practices and approaches to health issues, the practice of medicine in the far eastern societies of China, Japan and related countries have issues of practices that cannot be scientifically authenticated. Visits to shrines in Japan often seem to indicate a belief in the world of spirits and some form of paganism. Shrines however, are not foreign to the Buddhist religion and may not have much in common with the African perception of the word Shrine.

Undisputedly different are societies of India, Bangladesh, Sri Lanka, etc. in Asia Minor. Here too the practice of paganism stands far more in the forefront of social consciousness with the peasant folks than it is in far eastern societies. The production of Talisman to confront one social or spiritual ill or the other as well the belief in multi-deity is a casual stock in trade.

What all these societies – with the exception of the likes of Haiti – seem to have in common however, appears to be a perceptible dose of the involvement of the elements of science in their practice, if science is seen in the very limited sense of cognitive and rational perception. The public practice of paganism in Centers in Brazil for instance, serves to reduce the sense of awe and mystery attached to the perception when a Priest does not pretend to live and interact with forces in a different world in some clandestine coven beyond cognitive perception. A Priest is seen only as a Medium through which perceptions are transmitted to the ordinary man, whose sense of perception does not exceed the scientifically authenticated "five senses". Even though ultimately scientifically unverifiable, the human mind may be prone to live with such a reality much more comfortably than with a self-proclaimed 'Witch' that will or may transmit more details of outstanding issues only after the next night session in a mysterious coven.

In the next chapter we will strive to illustrate how the African perception, practice of and involvement in paganism, fetishism and animism plays out against such acts in other parts of the world. We will proceed thereafter, to reason on the impact of all such movements on the development of mind and soul as well as the society at large with a clear insight into the strategic position of Africa today with its own values in the developmental scheme of things on a global plane.

* * * * *

Chapter 2

Witchcraft and Sorcery as Understood in Sub-Saharan Africa!

Much like in the western world, the average African's conception of witchcraft is that of evil. The modern day understanding of pitching "Black Witchcraft" against "White Witchcraft" with the former symbolizing evil and the latter the fight against evil is also not unknown to the African psyche. In the overall weighting however, this differentiation is lesser pronounced in the African mentality than it is in several other parts of the world. In the evaluation and perception of witchcraft however, the rest of the world seems to have quite a lot in common with Africa.

The physically visualized image of a witch in Africa is by and large, also that of a flying human with such supernatural powers as enables it to perpetrate harmful spells on its surroundings and environs. In most parts of Africa, witchcraft is ordinarily associated with the powers of the night, literally meaning the power of darkness. In the Southern Nigerian language of "Edo", witches are often referred to as "Elders of the Night". They are generally assumed to depart from the physical consciousness of their own bodies in times of sleep. The entity that is assumed to sneak out of the human body during sleep is regarded as invisible and non-perceivable to the normal five senses of the non-initiated. This entity with wings that enables it to fly through the air, then proceeds to the coven – the ultimate meeting point of initiated witches – where deliberations are held, evil rituals performed and tasks assigned often to seal the fate of unsuspecting fellow humans who are the assumed victims. Such is one commonly held belief. What stands out most notably in the African understanding of witchcraft is the least emphasis on gender. A witch or sorcerer is not necessarily predominantly feminine. It could be very much a male as much as female. It could be young. It could be old and the old is much easier to profile as a potential witch.

The concept of flying reminds me of narratives in the books of Tuesday Lobsang Rampa – the controversial British self-styled Esoteric and Mystic. This purported documentary representation of far eastern mysticism talks about the Astral body, which leaves the physical body in times of sleep and is able to transcend the confining obstacles of time, space and mind.

Tuesday Lobsang Rampa, was born as Cyril Henry Hoskin in Plympton, Devon in 1910.[29] He claimed in several books authored by him before his death in 1981 that his physical body was taken over by the astral body or spirit of Lobsang Rampa from Tibet, in some transmigration of the soul after Rampa's body had become too worn to continue his mission on earth. On the assumption that the claims contained in the books authored under the name of Tuesday Lobsang Rampa truly reflect the beliefs and practices of mysticism in the Far East, it will be seen that Far Eastern mysticism regards those attributes which equate witchcraft (in the African understanding) as attributes that are shared by and inherent in all human beings.

It may be of interest to observe in a footnote at this juncture that all those "esoteric" claims and teachings so skillfully presented by Tuesday Lobsang Rampa in all his 19 books were vehemently challenged by accusations of fraud and willful deception. In fact, Lobsang Rampa was repeatedly accused by the British Press of being a Charlatan and a Con Artist. Accusations which ultimately prompted him to flee England in the 1960s to live the rest of his life in Canada where he died on January 25, 1981 at the age of 70![30]

With the slight difference that the astral body portrayed by Lobsang Rampa does not have wings[31] and simply floats through space and penetrates objects irrespective of their thickness, the similarity to the African witch is in the locomotion. Both entities are believed to leave the physical body only during somnian retreat. While Rampa portrays the image of an astral body that is linked to the physical body by an endlessly long sort of umbilical cord, the African conception of the witch leaving the body on somnian retreat is basically believed to fly with wings. Experiences made in such astral travels are described by Rampa as the human dream experience. Lobsang Rampa narrates that humans have the in-built ability (if they are able to go through and sustain the rigors of several years of disciplined and anti-materialist training in meditations and submission to nature) to make and even control such astral travels consciously and at will.[31] Astral Travel, according to these teachings, makes up only a trivial segment of what Far Eastern mysticism represents and seeks to impart on mankind.

The big dividing line however lies in the judgmental valuation of good and evil. While the notion of evil powers in connection with astral travel does not come up at all in Rampa's narratives (it is in fact, a non-issue altogether) and astral travel is portrayed as an attribute shared by all humans, witchcraft in Africa is believed to be predominantly about evil forces and not a general attribute that all humans have. Everybody is not a witch and witches are members of an ultimate and awesome secret and evil society.

This belief by the average African is expressed in various mundane forms. A simple deep sleep, from which the sleeper has difficulties waking up when a fellow man seeks to get him up quickly in the event of an emergency, is almost always sufficient to suspect the sleeping party of being a witch or sorcerer. The reasoning being the assumption that the astral body of the sleeper is yet in the middle of a coven session unable to return to the physical body so quickly! In some cases, the sleeper may even find himself/herself facing accusations of being the underlying evil force behind such an emergency if the emergency was a misfortune.

The Role of Witchcraft in the African Society

The subject of witchcraft in present-day African society is one serious reality that dominates daily life across all spectra. In the absence of any single perceivable and objective criterion for identifying a witch or sorcerer, the folks who overwhelmingly believe in the real existence of witches and witchcraft are guided by subjective, irrational and often arbitrary criteria.

Reporting on the origin of the Celtic tradition of Halloween, history books have consistently drawn a clear parallel between the agriculture-based natural life of the peasant folks of those early centuries in the region of Halloween's origin and the attachment of the folks to a belief in the world of spirits for harvest and life's occurrences.[14] Precisely this dependence of the African folk on the "volatile natural world" devoid of regular electricity and very many other social amenities regarded in more advanced societies as a matter of course is the identical characteristic that the African generally shares with the Celtic folks of those early centuries. It seems to explain the stronger leaning of the African today, towards the spirit world and the world of witchcraft.

It therefore goes by implication that the more rural or village communities in Africa with more routine occupation in forests, farms, rivers and lives in natural-structured houses of mud walls and thatched roofs have more in common with the "volatile natural world" than the metropolitan downtown gangster of Detroit city. These rural people are the folks, for whom every weird sound in the forest, every faltering step in the farm and every slip on the riverside is more likely to be subjected to metaphysical interpretations than the folks in big cities with the teeming hustle-bustle of bus rides and traffic congestion.

While the threshold for the palpable perception of witchcraft in the life of these two folks – rural versus urban – may differ in intensity, a comparison with countries of the western world seems realistically worlds apart.

Children and the Elderly

The village of Ikpe Ikot Nkon with which we began this discourse will serve us once again at this juncture as an exemplary case study. Most often, it takes a self-proclaimed animist Priest claiming clairvoyance and supernatural powers in consultation with oracles to identify or proclaim anyone in the local community as a rampaging evil witch to truly make a real palpable witch of any neighbor. What this means in a small village community can be best imagined amongst folks that have lived all their lives believing strongly in the evils of witchcraft. Being a witch or sorcerer means in this context, being forced to bear responsibility for sundry evil acts that have been visited on the community such as illnesses, death and other misfortunes. In the absence of hospitals and qualified doctors, fetish priests and voodoo experts bear the primary responsibility for administering treatment on patients often by exorcizing evil spirits from afflicted persons. Poor harvest seasons may often end up being conceived as the mischief of an evil witch or the handiwork of the spirit of one departed soul or the other. Sicknesses that are proving difficult to heal through fetish exorcism, will often translate into a more intensified effort to fish out the evil force or witch from the community, who is assumed to be perpetrating the evil on the neighborhood and finally neutralizing (meaning killing) him/her "spiritually" or physically once and for all if and when identified.

In some cases, it may even suffice to have had the witches identified in dreams. Confirmation by a fetish priest of the accuracy of any such dream after consultation with oracles in any small rural and even sometimes, urban community may mean the ultimate death sentence for an unsuspecting 'suspect'. The case even gains more legitimacy if it is the Priest himself revealing his own dreams or communication with the world beyond.

Such was the irrationality and arbitrariness that determined and sealed the fate of 95 year old Ukpong Uyong on October 08, 2011 in Ikpe Ikot Nkon in Southern Nigeria.

Ukpong Uyong was *"accused of using wizardry to plaque many with sicknesses and misfortunes"*. This prompted the emergency convention of an assembly at the village square in which the death sentence was pronounced on the old man without much ado. He was then *"beaten to death by irate youths of the small community"* at the village square.[2] It did not matter how verifiable or not the accusation was. It did not matter how credible or not the accuser or accusers was/were. The man was murdered in cold blood and the community saw absolutely no injustice in this diabolic act of jungle justice. Only his family and loved ones were left to cry out in defense of the departed soul. Helplessly too! There is a huge doubt though that this same family coming out in defense of the deceased who is also their loved one would have come out in such staunchness as well, if any of their own was the sick one for whom someone else had been identified and held responsible as the witch or sorcerer masterminding the misfortune. But this is yet just one single symptom of the great diabolical entrapment of mind and soul in the quest for intellectual development in African communities.

The clearly identifiable pattern in the African practice is a focus mostly, on elderly people and children.

The story of children being at the center of witchcraft accusations in Nigeria came to the limelight in the year 2010 when the American Cable Network News (CNN) featured a prominent story on the subject and reported on it from Southern Nigeria. The scene was Akwa Ibom. Unfortunately however, it was not a one-off case. There are countless other communities elsewhere in Africa that can testify to a similar pattern of the diabolical persecution of unsuspecting individuals.

Investigating on behalf of CNN, Christian Purefoy visited a Southern Nigerian Community to witness firsthand, the ostracization of two brothers and sisters being cast out of their immediate family and the village community at large, by their own mother. She accused the children of causing the premature death of two of their own siblings through their magical powers in clairvoyance. There was no persuading her that this cannot be true.

In such a conventional African setting, which some may choose to describe as primitive, it hardly matters that other progressive societies such as in

Europe and elsewhere would have taken a different approach. They would have tried the scientific method of probing into and analyzing the cause of infant mortality with a view to finding lasting socio-political solutions. The traditional African mind will however, prefer to adopt the analytical option perpetrated by a fetish priest consulting some invisible and non-existent forces through the power of dubious oracles.

Sam Ikpe Itauma of the Child's Rights and Rehabilitation Network tried to convince the mother of these children that there could be no truth to the claim of her children being sorcerers who were behind the premature death of two of their own siblings. Unsuccessfully!

"I am afraid. They are witches and they can kill me as well" The mother was quoted as saying.[32]

The kids had already been surrounded by a village crowd as is typical in the public identification of suspected witches by so-called 'spiritual' methods that are devoid of all scientific and rationally comprehensible verifications. Sam Itauma had to take the kids with him to his Orphanage.

"If we are not here there's a possibility of them being thrown into the river, buried alive or stabbed to death"[32]

Purefoy reports that Sam Itauma runs an orphanage that houses about 200 children all accused of witchcraft and cast out by their own family. Some unlucky victims are tortured often through beating, burning with boiling water, machete cuts etc. to their untimely death. Sam Itauma reports another emotionally compelling story of a 5-year old boy. The boy who he called Godwin had lost his mother at that tender age of 5. Unfortunately, it was a local Pastor who saw some 'vision' that declared Godwin a witch who held him responsible for the death of his own mother. The inevitable had to happen as often in such circumstances: Ostracization to the point of death! After the initial denial of being a sorcerer, Godwin was beaten mercilessly until he confessed to witchcraft.[32] In fact, until he too was probably made to believe that he was truly a witch with this extraordinary power over the life and death of people around him! The role of Pastors and Christian Preacher Men in this diabolic scheme will be revisited in more detail as this discourse progresses.

In the final analysis, it is not uncommon that children often end up truly believing themselves to have been evil sorcerers having experienced gruesome processes culminating in the confession of witchcraft. Fantastic confessional accounts narrated in the aftermath of coercion as far as the human senses can perceive, are taken as detailed admissions of this weird diabolic act.

Nigeria is reported to have adopted the Child Rights Law only as recently as the year 2003. The aim of domesticating this international convention to safeguard the rights of children and protect them against the torturous impact of this evil branding should have been a paramount motive in the passage of this law by the Nigerian Central government. In the Nigerian political setting, the practical implementation of this law will move closer to realization only after regional legislatures have ratified and enacted the law for local enforcement. As of June 2011 however, media reports indicate that only 16 out the total of 36 States in the country have made this law a part of their regional legislative identity.[33]

As recently as the year 2008 - again in the Nigerian State of Akwa-Ibom – a Pastor bearing the title of a Bishop and named Sunday Williams declared that the entire state was a coven for witches. He stated unequivocally that the state was awash with roughly 2.3 million witches most of whom are children. [33] The State of Akwa-Ibom is said to be having a population of roughly 4 million people. His source and the method of scientific investigation applied in the provision of this statistical figure however remained a highly guarded secret for "Bishop Sunday Williams". Most interesting is the fact that this assertion was reportedly made under the full gaze of representatives of the International News media. Sunday Williams boasted of having killed up to 110 such child witches. He had charged and probably still charges as much as 40,000 Naira (about €200.00) to help willing parents kill their own children as long as they have been branded witches with evil forces. Some of these children are from stepmothers' homes.[33]

The Elders

More brutally exposed to this arbitrary regime of social profiling and branding are often elderly people. Traditions in several countries and cultures in Africa have one element in common. They are hierarchy-based. Hierarchy is generally driven by respect for age. Age stands for wisdom, experience and wealth in the awesomeness of life beyond the comprehension of youthfulness.

It therefore goes that the elderly are traditionally respected and held in high esteem not for the numbers that their age represent (because in most cases, many old people at least until recently, hardly have clear-cut proof of their real age with births unregistered and Birth Certificates unknown at the time of their birth) but more for the sense of awesomeness that their multiple accumulation of dermal wrinkles transmit to the young and tender ones growing out of natural innocence. Elders are indeed sources of knowledge and bearers of historical tidings. In the absence of western education, elders were the only sources known for the reliable transmittance of oral history. It becomes a matter of course that knowledge of this sort is often automatically equated with wisdom and a sense of awesomeness.

Apart from being seen to possess wisdom in a miniature god-like perception, the Elderly in Africa is often treated almost as a valuable cultural asset. He is assumed to be embodying natural clairvoyance and some affiliation with perceptions in the life beyond. These qualities are often deemed acquired in the course of several years of personal journey through life. Journeys deemed invaluable and non-purchasable! That is as far as elemental African Tradition goes. Several centuries and generations of transformation have however taken their toll on the present day manifestation of the hierarchy-based aspect of African tradition.

Inter-personal exchange of honor and respect based on age is no doubt one element that still continues to dominate daily life in every community in Africa till our present day. The fact however that the unwritten law about old people's subliminal abilities also invokes a sense of fear in the mind of the undiscerning neophyte in the journey through life is one natural phenomenal reaction. In a transformed world that is successfully boosting self-assertion and confidence through education and religious diversity however, fears are handled in differing ways and means. The perception of the *"Elders of the night"* is thus subjected to some mental processing and understanding based on the basic identity of the community in question with all attendant social attributes.

It is not unusual in several African communities today, to profile long-living elders as gaining their extended years in life at the expense of younger victims. I have personally been privy to narrations in my neighborhood in my childhood days, about elderly persons living long (presumably over 100 years), by sacrificing the lives of younger people through diabolic arrangements in covens. It is usually assumed and narrated in rural and some urban communities that individual witches commit themselves to diverse obligations in their mysterious coven meetings. The fulfillment of such obligations is deemed to facilitate ascension in ranks and generally enhance elevated status. This includes the number of years that the individual may wish to live. An elderly person is therefore almost always a potential target of profiling as a murderer upon the death of any young person in the neighborhood. Should this suspicion also end up being confirmed by any other self-proclaimed witch with the self-proclaimed power of clairvoyance, it will almost certainly mean the lynching of the unsuspecting elder.

The enhanced status of being associated with supernatural powers often manifest in the general avoidance of and show of respect for perceived elderly witches. As if in a seeming attempt to utilize and take due advantage of this elevated social status, a dominant number of fetish Priests are often elderly people.

Part of the uniqueness of the position of elders is their responsibility in passing over knowledge from generation to generation such as identifying herbs and medicinal plants for the healing and treatment of illnesses. For such elders involved in the business of clairvoyance and fetishism however, this warrants the modification of the designation "Fetish Priest" to the more acceptable phrase "Native Doctor" to denote usefulness and service to humanity. It therefore becomes easier for an elderly person to come out openly and boast of being a Native Doctor rather than Witch. The latter being a phrase that would provoke immediate lynching. A native doctor then finds it easier to proclaim witchcraft in his/her practices emphasizing commitment to service to humanity rather than the destruction of human lives. Within the confines of private practice however, it will not be unusual to find individual clients buying destructive services precisely from the same 'native doctors'.

A jealous woman sensing a rival woman competing with her for the affection of the same man would usually pay for a native doctor's intervention to get rid of the rival. This would often involve request for death, illness or any other form of misfortune upon the rival. I remember a recent case in my own vicinity, of a lady soliciting a native doctor's service to inflict madness or mental illness on her ex-boyfriend for making up his mind to settle with a rival lady rather than herself. The same applies to the elimination of rivals at workplaces, career enhancements and all sorts of life challenges. When misfortunes strike in such cases, they are usually termed "spiritual misfortunes".

Any casual road accident may thus qualify as a spiritual accident engineered and remote-controlled by some witches at the service of rivals and competitors. Hardly any death or illness is accepted by a typical African as natural. Even sick people who seek treatment in hospitals will engage the parallel service of a "Native Doctor" to help identify and dismiss the evil spirit behind the ailment. Church goers will resort to fasting and prayer for the exorcism of the imagined evil spirit often suspected to be someone in the neighborhood.

For the elderly therefore, it is also often a matter of honor to be viewed in awe and some distant consternation, as an entity in possession of unusual supernatural powers. It is not unusual to find elders who will gladly showcase themselves as positive witches helping humanity to fight against prevalent evil forces. It is like the proverbial saying of everyone talking about fighting crime but no one agreeing to being the criminal.

Elder Shara Oboh is aged 98. He is the land owner of one of Nigeria's luxurious holiday resorts – The Obudu Mountain Ranch. A vacation complex located in Cross River State at the Obudu Plateau at an altitude of 1,700 meters above sea level close to the Nigerian border with Cameroon! At the advanced age of 98 Shara Oboh is described as a rare breed of the human race for his physical features that have simply refused to crumble under the weight of age. *"He can stand straight upright, talk for hours on end, he sees clearly and hears clearly without the need of an hearing aid, one can conveniently say that at 98, Oboh has the energy of a 30-year-old."* a local newspaper reports. In 2010, he married a 25 year-old girl named Christiana as his fourth wife. Nine months later, he fathered a baby boy. While the newspaper reports that visitors to Obudu sincerely doubt the paternity of the new-born baby boy, members of Oboh's extended family and local villagers hold Shara Oboh in a profound sense of awe.[34]

At 98, he is able to perform what youths do at more tender ages and his admirers attribute this to supernatural powers. For a start, the salient fact is negated that births were hardly registered in those old days in Africa in which the old man was born. Much like he will be unable to provide a valid birth certificate to prove his age, there will hardly be any credible person alive to testify that the man is truly likely to be 98 years old. Nevertheless, the story readily calls to mind the case of the 94-year old Indian Ramajit Raghav, who was widely reported to have fathered a healthy baby-boy born by his wife, the 50-year-old Shakuntala Raghav in December 2010. A feat that he repeated again on October 05, 2012 now aged 96 and his wife 52.[35] This earned Raghav the title of the oldest father alive as proclaimed by the Times of India basically on the strength of irrefutable proof of age. Like Oboh who is reportedly 4 years older, the Indian Raghav was also declared to have been as sexually active as a 25-year old individual. In contrast to the Nigerian Shara Oboh however, no supernatural attribute was mentioned in India. Similar cases in Turkey that I remember date back however to a few decades. They were reports of elderly men fathering children at highly advanced ages. Never were references made to supernatural attributes.

Shara Oboh is even ready and happy to subscribe to the fact that he has supernatural powers. *"My*

*power is positive, it is not negative. I catch witches
and other classes of evil doers. My power is what I call
supernatural power from God. ... I use my God-given
power to catch thieves, witches, wizards and other evil
doers. When they see me they panic, because they know I
have superior power. It is true that when I was young,
many villagers ran away from me because they considered
me an evil spirit that could kill but they have accepted
me, they know my power is positive."*[(34)]

The bottom line is clear. As long as his powers are
not declared evil, it is easy to boast of possessing the
power of subliminal perception.

The story changes however, when relatives begin
to develop ideas. Should an immediate or extended
family member or anyone in the neighborhood be
afflicted by any long-standing illness and some
adventure-loving "Native Doctor" decides to see the
fingers of the elderly family member in the affliction,
admiration will quickly turn to abhorrence. Fear will
make way for the urge to destroy. Then, instrumental
worshippers of Christ will begin to chant Hallelujah
and mobilize their 'salvation army' armed with the
"Holy Ghost fire"!

Most pathetic is the situation of ailing elders
suffering Alzheimer and other forms of deterioration
in mental health. Any random mention by any
such individual, of having practiced witchcraft or
declaration of responsibility for the death of anyone
within the family or in the entire neighborhood will
often not be attributed to the failing mental health

of the elderly person. It will be celebrated as a major confession of spiritual crime and evil deeds.

As in many similar circumstances, there will almost be nothing to hang onto by such an elderly individual if he/she is dependent on care by family members. There is a minimum of one case known to me in person, in which an old woman in this category was tied to a wood in a room in an uncompleted building by her own children. It happened sometimes in the 1970s and no one can swear that it does not happen today anymore. The old woman who had suddenly suffered a mental breakdown had gone naked and broke out of the house narrating weird stories of witchcraft and evil things that she had purportedly been responsible for. In her incarceration in the uncompleted building she was only sparsely cared for getting meals at the whims and caprices of her tormentors and left to wallow in her own urine and fecal ejections. I often heard her children express satisfaction and swear at her for all the evils she is perceived to have done as purportedly confirmed by her own "confessions".

Having worked as an old peoples' nurse on part-time basis as a student in Europe, I have witnessed a lot of heavily-weighted statements made by incurable patients of Alzheimer in Old Peoples' Homes. Never are such words taken as confessions and never are the people subjected to inhuman treatments on the strength of statements they have made out of mental incapacitation.

It should also be added at this juncture that the Alzheimer disease, which today, is commonly diagnosed in Europe and America (following intensive scientific research to ascertain and define the nature of the disease) is not a household phenomenon in the African world of medical research or medical care. On the contrary, there is hardly any awareness of the existence of such a disease among the general public. Even the academia seems locked in a state of denial that Alzheimer exists in Africa. Indeed, one recent joint USA/Nigerian study carried out by Dr. Hugh Hendrie of the department of Psychiatry and Medicine in Indiana University's School of Medicine, Indianapolis, USA and Dr. Andesola Ogunniyi of the University of Ibadan, Nigeria, and released in 2001 emphatically posited that the *"Rates of Alzheimer's disease are lower in Africans living in Africa than in African Americans"*.[36]

This was even outreached by the results of a pilot study conducted in South Africa and released in March 2009 which seems to strengthen the belief that the Alzheimer disease is basically a white man's disease that has nothing to do with the Blackman.

Analyzing these awry findings of the pilot study though, one Dr. Jopie de Beer strikes a reasonable note on the circumstances of self-delusion underlying such conclusions:

"The truth however, might be that dementia is just severely under-diagnosed and dementia-related symptoms are ascribed to common causes ("elderly are like that") or witchcraft. This prevents sufferers of dementia

and their caregivers from getting the necessary medical attention and social support...[(37)] This indeed, is the true position supported by realities on the ground.

Yet it is difficult to pass this message of proper reflection on to many people within diverse African communities. Experiences for which the services of mental healthcare experts are usually sought elsewhere in the world are often stigmatized in Africa as products of forces from a world beyond our perception.

Sundry Manifestation of Superstition and Elemental Metaphysics

As in all other civilizations, superstition in Africa also takes many different forms. Owls are for instance, generally believed to be human witches who have simply taken the temporary form of the bird. Cats (not just black cats as in many European beliefs) are generally associated with an aggravated level of clairvoyance and therefore seen as one instrument used by human witches for temporary transformation. The pawpaw tree, the gigantic and almost formidable looking iroko tree and the middle of road intersections are generally regarded as coven locations for the nighttime meetings of witches after leaving their physical bodies. A pawpaw tree once branded in this respect will be allowed to blossom abundantly and abandoned untouched. It may yield the most delicious and attractive possible fruits. It will be left untouched and people will look the other way rather than enjoying the product of nature in consumption or commercial marketing.

Physical signs are also taken seriously in the interpretation of superstitious messages. A sudden physical cramp on the leg may be taken as a brisk spiritual warning interpreted for the relevant meaning depending on which of the legs is affected. It may also apply to the arms.

Dreams are the most commonly used source of interpreting *spiritual* messages. An unsuspecting neighbor, relation, friend or co-staff may wake up one morning to realize that he is suddenly being avoided and sometimes subjected to outright aggressive and unfriendly behavior from someone close to him simply because he had been seen 'in a bad light' in a dream. Often a parent, sibling or friend may simply call to warn against unguarded friendship and interaction with any other third party simply because this parent, sibling or friend may have seen the third party in a dream also 'in a bad light'. This often paves the way for suspicion of witchcraft and other forms of evil powers. Children are consequently warned to avoid any such suspect while visits and other expression of friendliness are suddenly curtailed for reasons unknown to the person who was seen in a dream. The situation may even escalate if the health of any of the suspecting party coincidentally deteriorates.

Stern supporters of Pan-Africanist thinking will defend this act and claim it to have been the primordial science of our ancestors, which did not hamper survival without the aid of advanced technology. They will negate the fact of the irrationality of dreams. They will quickly refer to the cross-cultural universality of the belief in dream interpretation. They will underscore the fact that the African is not alone in this act.

In his book "The Interpretation of Dreams", the doyen of Psychoanalysis Sigmund Freud, wrote that dreams are "...*disguised fulfillment of represented wishes*".[38] Indeed, Freud held the views that dreams were nothing but a representation of our unconscious desires, thoughts and motivations. He regards these emotional processes as creeping into our dreams because they are not consciously expressed. That is as far as Psychoanalysis goes.

In reference to the book "Sleep" by J. A. Hobson, Kendra Cherry wrote the followings:

"The activation–synthesis model of dreaming was first proposed by J. Allan Hobson and Robert McClarley in 1977. According to this theory, circuits in the brain become activated during REM sleep, which causes areas of the limbic system involved in emotions, sensations and memories, including the amygdala and hippocampus, to become active. The brain synthesizes and interprets this internal activity and attempts to find meaning in these signals, which results in dreaming. This model suggests that dreams are a subjective interpretation of signals generated by the brain during sleep."[39]

Indeed, while science is still working to establish a credible understanding of the dreaming process, realities have been established in human behavior underscoring a sharp departure from irrational dream interpretation to a more realistic and science-based regulation of daily lives. Societies in other continents in which this tendency has been better consolidated have come a long, hard way. Rationality is now more widely accepted as a way of confronting life's multifaceted difficulties in such societies. They have left behind them the interpretation of dreams as a means of influencing activities in human life. In fact such attitudes have been dropped as historical ballasts largely treated today in blessed memory as primordial values of the ancestors. Coincidentally too, all such societies seem to maintain a higher level of advancement with all its attendant impacts on social welfare and education as opposed to several African societies.

Rural communities in Asia and South America sharing these characteristic values with African societies often also appear to have other negative social attributes in common with their African counterparts. Lower levels of education, lower levels of income and stronger beliefs in religion, superstition and metaphysics are just a few of such attributes, which make rational observers embrace the notion of a possible complicated network of cause-effect relationships underlying the progression and development of the individual attributes and characteristic values.

Metaphysics is in fact, nothing new. It is indeed nothing else than a philosophical inclination towards the clarification of the huge unanswered question hovering above the concept of being and knowing. In fact, some sources describe metaphysics as the relation between the Universals and the Particulars, "the teleological doctrine of causation".[40] Probing into metaphysics often uncovers the sometimes, blurred boundary between Philosophy and Religion. It uncovers the universality of human beliefs. Beliefs that are shaped by the diverse forms of education beginning from parental upbringing through teachings at schools at various levels to learning in casual social interactions! In other words, the role of metaphysics, religion or philosophy in our daily lives is often shaped and modified by a dose of social education that may define the particularity and peculiarity of any given society.

While superstitious beliefs and metaphysics both play their roles in daily lives in every society, the pervasiveness of beliefs and the seriousness accorded to such beliefs in daily lives often also plays a role in defining the value of informal education in shaping the quality of beliefs. While I proceed at this juncture on the understanding that formal education in schools and universities goes a long way in enhancing intellectual development, I will endeavor to also acknowledge its complementary function to parental education and education through casual social interactions.

In societies like the African in general and Nigerian in particular, where in spite of widespread formal education in schools and universities, education through casual social interaction still seems to play a major role among people, beliefs in superstition are highly significant to the life of the individual. With the elements of fear, awe and admiration that they contain, they are transferred from persons to persons, from groups to groups in almost every facet of daily interaction. They are ductile and thrive on willful docility. The expression of such beliefs agitates emotions, modifies them in helpless designs and leaves them searching for the ultimate redemption by powers beyond the realms of normal perception. The weapon of choice is often "primordial instincts" tapping on elemental human fear. The fear of the unknown! For the purpose of this discourse, we choose the label "Elemental Metaphysics" to describe this near-collective state of social submission. It is elemental in view of its confinement to the rudimentary principles of the start of time. It seems to embody a virtual refusal to transform with the tide of times and an adamant adherence to values that are erroneously and unselectively believed to have *"stood the test of time"* without discarding the attendant failed entities and dark sides of such ominous values.

In other words, while superstition and fear of the unknown is nothing peculiar to the African society, the pervasiveness of superstition in the daily life of a black African individual underscores the social significance of superstition in the continent as a whole.

The causes are indeed, easy to identify in political, economic and other forms of mismanagement. Our purpose in this discourse however, is not a causative exploration but a teleological analysis of where the exacerbated and hyped superstitious values have left the African society today with a clear focus on the failure of formal education to uplift the mind of individuals in pursuit of social psychological development. A situation that clearly contrasts with other societies that have come a long way from similar social-psychological attributes in the history of mankind!

Human Sacrifice

The early days of tribal lives in primordial rural and natural Africa no doubt had their idyllic touch of serenity and harmony with the elements of basic existence. Unfortunately, the concept of human sacrifice for one spiritual appeasement or the other was not an uncommon dark side of this undisputable serenity and unison with nature. It is just one whimsical example of the attributes of destructive superstition that the undiscerning African still chooses to retain in some aspects of social life from primordial times. Stories of so-called "Ritualists" kidnapping people to kill and sacrifice to different types of gods to enhance private wishes and aspirations, are not uncommon to Nigerian news media even today.

Human sacrifice in ancient Africa served different purposes depending on the ethnic group and the aim to be achieved. There have always been reports in history, reaching from ancient Egypt down to the Bantu regions of Black Africa, of kings who died and were never buried alone. Slaves and other 'live belongings' had to be buried with them. In some cases, such 'live belongings' were suspected to have been buried alive.

Caroline Seawright recounts that *"there is some evidence that human sacrifice may have been practiced in the Nile Valley during the 1ˢᵗ Dynasty and possibly also in Pre-dynastic Egypt"*[41]

Writing on October 11, 2003, she quotes Jacques Kinnaer's "Human Sacrifice" saying that *"the earliest known example of human sacrifice may perhaps be found in pre-dynastic burials in the south of Egypt, dated to the Naqada II period. One of the discovered bodies showed marks of the throat from having been cut before being decapitated"*.[41]

Seawright further recalls that sacrifice to gods was just one form of human sacrifices suspected to have been practiced in Egypt. This may have required the slaying of criminals or prisoners of war. The aim being:

- *"The ritual killing of human beings as part of the offerings presented to the gods on a regular basis, or on special occasions.*

- *Retainer sacrifice, or the killing of domestic servants to bury them along with their master."* (Jacques Kinnaer)[41]

Moving geographically downwards into the Bantu region of Sub-Saharan Africa, documentations are more difficult to come by. A large part of ancient African history that is known to the world today is based on oral transmission passed down through generations or eye witness accounts by colonial explorers.

It is on this basis that information was released to the outside world of the widespread practice of human sacrifice in Sub-Saharan Africa particularly in countries along the West African coast and further inland. As in ancient Egypt, human sacrifice in West Africa also served the purpose of either pleasing or appeasing the gods, spirits or dead people's souls. It was much like the ritual slaughtering of animals that was hardly ever called into question. Retainer sacrifices served the purpose of killing servants and slaves for a dead king or queen to enable the monarchs retain their 'private properties' that will continue to serve them in the life beyond.

Gods, spirits and the souls of the deceased were basically appeased or appealed to in times of famine, poor harvest, epidemy, war, disasters and other forms of tribulation in reminiscence of the Celts' dependence on the 'volatile natural world' 2000 years ago in triggering the Halloween. The most common times of human sacrifice however were times in which a king or queen passed away. Wikipedia recalls

Dahomey (today's Republic of Benin), the former Benin Empire (with its remnant core now known as Benin City in South Midwestern Nigeria) and Ghana as the most notorious examples in West Africa. R. J. Rummel recounts that *"hundreds, sometimes even thousands, of prisoners would be slain"* when a ruler died in the grand Dahomean custom. *"In one of these ceremonies in 1727, as many as 4,000 were reported killed. In addition, Dahomey had an Annual Custom during which 500 prisoners were sacrificed."*[42]

The consolidation of Islam in the northern parts of West Africa through the Trans-Saharan Trade led to the earlier eradication of this nauseating practice from the northern region. European colonial infiltration further downwards facilitated initial foreign observation of this indigenous African culture. Some sources recount that European explorers were initially not much interested in intervening or interfering in the African practice of human sacrifice since they very much resembled executions known to the travelers in their home countries. It was however the gradual influx of Christian Missionaries deep into Africa that began to awaken a sense of resentment and the campaign to drive home the awareness of the barbaric implication of this senseless act of killing fellow humans for an unknown life beyond perception. When the act was successfully challenged and tabooed beyond open practice, oral accounts report of a continued underground and secret practice of the act even deep into the 19th century. Mary Slessor's campaign against the killing of twins in Nigeria's Calabar in the early 20th century can then be understood to have been just a tip of the iceberg.

In fact, there are records indicating beyond doubt that the practice of human sacrifice was not peculiar to the African continent. Even though Africa was about the last bastion of this barbaric and inhuman act, Wikipedia recounts the practice of human sacrifice in Mesopotamia, Levant, Phoenecia, Neolithic Europe, Greco-Roman Antiquity, The Celts, The Germanic Peoples, Slavic People, China, Tibet, India, The Pacific region, Pre-Columbian Americas, etc.[43] The forms differed from region to region. Today however, the concept of human sacrifice in almost all of these regions except in Africa is a thing of history recounted only on the pages of history books. Precisely this painful reality characterizes Africa's status of being left behind in almost every facet of human development and national advancement.

As recently as January 07, 2012, the British Telegraph carried the headline *"Human Sacrifices 'on the rise in Uganda' as witch doctors admit to rituals"*[44]. The activities of so-called "Ritualists" are not uncommon in Nigeria and many other African countries. Complete humans or human parts are required for religious sacrifices and rituals often to enhance political ambitions, acquire wealth, bear children, enhance good health or perform one supernatural wonder or the other such as rendering the human skin bulletproof, etc. For one reason or the other, millions of indigenous African folks believe in and hold on strongly to the authenticity of these inauspicious and often hilarious phenomena.

In Uganda, *"one man said he had clients who had captured children and taken their blood and body parts to his shrine, while another confessed to killing at least 70 people including his own son"* reports The Telegraph. [44]

This was echoed in a government outcry decrying the rising wave of human sacrifice in Uganda in the year 2010. Indeed this newspaper report was based on a BBC Newsnight program *"Uganda: Battling the Witch-Doctors"* that was screened on BBC2. [44]

A self-declared witch-doctor who confessed to having been paid 500,000 Ugandan Shillings (roughly £160.00 at the time) *"denied any direct involvement in murder or incitement to murder"* claiming that his spirits issued direct instructions to his clients on what to do and what they did included this:

"They ... capture other people's children. They bring the heart and the blood directly here to take to the spirits ... They bring them in small tins and they place these objects under the tree from which the voices of the spirits are coming." [44]

Records provided by Assistant Commissioner of Police Moses Binoga who headed the Ugandan Anti-Human Sacrifice and Trafficking Task Force claims that only three cases of sacrifice-related ritual killings were recorded in 2007. In 2009, this had surged dramatically to 26.

"We also have about 120 children and adults reported missing whose fate we have not traced ... From the experience of those whom we recovered, we cannot rule out that they may be victims of human sacrifice." he says.[44]

Reporting for the Nigerian Newswatch on August 16, 2004, Chris Ajaero authored an article titled *"The Confessions of Okija Shrine Priests"*. The report detailed a police raid on a dreaded animist shrine in a Nigerian town known as Okija. A place he describes as a *"sleepy and hilly community."*[45] For reasons based on influences over several years and perhaps decades, local folks in Okija – much like in other African cities – hold their shrines in absolute reverence. They often seek to receive *"spiritual relief"* from all forms of tribulations and life's unsolicited hardships and strongly believe in the realization of same.

Continuing, Chris Ajaero recounts in Newswatch that the police raid on two shrines in Okija on August 04th, 2004 ended up with the arrest of *"39 traditional shrine priests"* or self-proclaimed witch-doctors on allegation of multiple homicides. A minimum of 20 human skulls and one fresh corpse in a coffin were recovered from the shrines.

Reporting from Lagos on the same event, Reuters News Agency gave an account of 30 witch doctors arrested at the shrines where 50 decomposing bodies and 20 human skulls were discovered. Local police spokesman was quoted as saying that that the bodies were lying in coffins and some of the skulls were "*really fresh*"[(46)]

"*The heads, genitals and other vital parts of some of the bodies found in a teak forest in Okija village had been severed; a sign they may have been killed for ritual ... (in a country where) ... Ritual killing is common in some parts ... where many people believe they can become instant millionaires by using human organs to make potent charms.*"[(46)]

These findings naturally ignited fear of the clandestine practice of human sacrifice in the shrines involved.

OKIJA SHRINE WITH A CORPSE IN THE
MIDDLE AND HUMAN SKULLS AROUND

Explaining the discovery, interrogated shrine priests reported that the persons involved were not killed for human sacrifice. Findings were the mere *"remains of individuals struck dead by the deities"* for the evil deeds of such persons *"such as lying, greed and oppression of fellow human beings."*[45] The corpses had to be brought to the shrine to protect other relations of the deceased persons from further incurring the wrath of the gods from visiting more misfortune on them.

How much this explanation allayed fears stemming from the popular belief that human sacrifice had been practiced in the shrines remains an unanswered question.

One of the priests Edinmuo Ndukwu threw more light on the underlying belief in the powers of the gods. One of such gods is called Ogwugwu Isiula. [45] He explains that swearing falsely before this god results in the god striking the culprit dead. He claims that even though the priests of Okija shrines do not use human heads for rituals, the deities were capable of making people rich, women barren, etc.

Precisely these beliefs it is that form the background to the perception that people have of the shrines and their related deities. Patronage of the powers of such deities is not uncommon amongst the ordinary folks but also largely by politicians and elites of the ruling class.

* * * * *

Chapter 3

Deities and Shrines: The "Ayelala" Example of Exploiting Prostitution for Pecuniary Gains

Reports of weird practices prescribed by priests and witch-doctors as prerequisites for the attainment of fame, wealth, good health, power and victory over perceived foes and evil spirits, are not uncommon in media reports.

In fact today, the Internet is still home to pictures of two purported Nigerian politicians of Yoruba (western Nigerian) descent standing naked before animist shrines to swear to some oath administered in the pursuit of political ambitions.[47]

Even one of Nigeria's flamboyant and outspoken regional politicians, former Governor of Ogun State Mr. Gbenga Daniel was at the center of such controversies for several weeks and months in the year 2009. He was alleged to have been photographed naked while performing rituals before a shrine. A regional Legislator Mr. Tokunbo Oshin who found himself at loggerheads with the Governor over power struggle had boasted openly, of being in possession of such photographs allegedly showing the Governor in a naked pose before a shrine.[48] Indeed, another picture also circulated in the media on June 29, 2009 equally featured another regional legislator Mr. Olawale Alausa in nudity before an animist shrine in Ijebu-Igbo.[48]

Political recriminations can no doubt, be identified as the driving force behind these voluntary revelations of compromising photos. It is the actions of political opponents seeking to unmask the level of political dubiousness of their enemies. A level of probity that is hardly ever compatible with the high demands of political leadership! Each opponent pursues the aim of outplaying his counterpart every step of the way. The situation goes a very long way to uncover the extent to which this folly of irrational practices and belief in the power of gods and shrines holds the entire society to ransom even at the very top. It leaves a poser on the role played by gods, oracles, shrines and witch-doctors in important decisions reached by African leaders in ruling their various constituencies. This is most important against the backdrop of the vast number of people affected by decisions taken by such leaders. It also leaves a poser on the extent to which superstitious beliefs regulate interactions amongst such politicians. Today, several centuries after colonial intrusion, Africa still remains coincidentally, the sole non-starter in the race to make the world a better and more affluent home for humanity.

The belief that the gods, shrines and priests are sources of supernatural powers is a widespread phenomenon. Children grow up in different parts of Africa watching their parents and people in the neighborhoods enmeshed in the practical expression of such beliefs. They witness the performance of rituals before shrines, the chanting of incantations to invoke the spirits of gods and departed souls. They are subjected to minor mutilations of their skins (on the face, chest and back) using razor blades with the application of different substances on the cuts believing them to be the ultimate magical jelly beans endowing them with supernatural powers or protecting them from one evil or the other. The form of cut particularly on the face differ from region to region and the remnant scars when the cuts heal, served in ancient times as tribal marks for identifying the geographical origin of individuals.

One outstanding example of such gods and self-made deities in parts of Africa today is the Ayelala deity in Southern Nigeria's Benin City – former core of the Benin Kingdom.

The people of Benin City have witnessed several phases of organized cultist fraternities over several periods. Names like "Owegbe" and "Ogboni" have come and gone and continue to exist today only on the sideline of public consciousness as shadows of what they used to be. They were secret cults emphasizing the strength of fraternal bonds. Hardly anyone but members of the organizations knew precisely what transpired within the organizations behind closed doors. The secret cults have thrived on popular fear of the unknown over several decades, with some clad of mystery and assumed invincibility. Their members have been looked upon as holders of powers beyond the ordinary. Rumors have always flown around of weird and mysterious initiation ceremonies. This has always offered members of such cults the opportunity to bask in the glory of a widely assumed sense of spiritual superiority. There is a period in the history of political development, in which a military government summarily banned secret cults in Nigeria in the aftermath of glaring nonchalance.

Thereafter the cults were driven underground and their value dissipated with time. Today however, one deity that has remained unknown to several generations in spite of its long period of existence has resurged in public consciousness filling a psychological gap in a society that seems in constant need of spiritual guidance where all other rational forces of redemption have failed.

The Ayelala deity resurfaced from nowhere out of wanton necessity and has now grown into a sinister level of arbitrary notoriety.

Available records trace the origin of the Ayelala deity to Western Nigeria. Sources provide conflicting historical accounts of a woman who was killed in a western Nigerian community of Ilaje. One source reports human sacrifice as the underlying starting point. A southern Nigerian woman slave from a region called "Ijaw" who was sacrificed for some vicarious reasons had murmured the word "Ayelala" in pain and agony at the point of her death. The word is said to refer to the incomprehensibility and cruelty of the world we are living in. An obvious reference to the injustice surrounding her vicarious sacrifice! The lady was subsequently deified and the god named Ayelala.[49]

The obvious downward spiral in the level of affluence that greeted Nigerians in the aftermath of dwindling economic fortunes (which they enjoyed between the 1970s and early 1980s) saw a gradual return of many Nigerians to 'tried and tested' primordial values.

The late Nigerian Afrobeat musician Fela Anikulapo Kuti best exemplified the underlying philosophy of this primordial trend in several songs and actions. Even though he personally was not driven by want or economic deprivation, he was able to sow his philosophical seed of returning Africans to core African values, on a fertile soil that was failed by political leadership in providing credible alternatives. In the days of economic boom and heightened levels of affluence most notably in the mid to late 1970s, I witnessed a generation of youths that was gradually drifting away from several primitive elements of spiritism, occultism and lethal traditionalist tendencies. Aspects of the African tradition and culture that complemented science, modern medicine and values were gladly embraced as the leadership gradually moved the country towards such a healthy blend of academic and cultural education. As resources dwindled however and laboratories could no longer afford proper equipment and hospitals ran out of quality and qualified materials, spiritual renaissance began to gain more significance. After all, our ancestors lived and survived in primitive settings with primitive amenities before the coming of the white man. Fela Anikulapo Kuti of blessed memory would rely on messages of this sort urging his audience in captivating tunes, to embrace those things that the African soil can offer. But it offered no cure for AIDS, which ultimately claimed his own life.

The resurgence of the Ayelala deity had a blank of this sort that it had to fill.

There was also the surge in crime statistics (particularly homicide) underscoring insecurity to life and property. A corrupt justice system starting from the Police to the Courts suddenly saw the Ayelala shrine becoming a parallel location for the administration of justice in Benin City.

For reasons that are yet to be subjected to serious scientific investigations, the Ayelala deity resurged to fame in Benin City roughly two decades ago. It is renowned for adjudicating cases ranging from witchcraft, land disputes, adultery, theft, etc. before a Chief Priest at the dreaded resident shrine of the Ayelala deity. Its trademark impact being the purported visiting of instant death upon the alleged guilty party in any dispute through abdominal swelling till the point of explosion! One Nigerian newspaper quoting an Ayelala Priest reports as follows:

"To evoke Ayelala deity … there must be a cock or duck, white cloth, seven needles, 7 parrot feathers, seven alligator peppers and seven native chalks. These ingredients will be concealed in the stomach of the cock or duck and wrapped with the white cloth. The cock will be eventually soaked in the Ayelala water and a curse will be pronounced on the evil doer. Chief Otedo told the Nigerian Observer that when the victim is caught by the deity he or she will swell as the cock or duck swells in the water."[50]

Since the administration of justice became a commodity for the highest bidder due to the corrupt justice system, the Nigerian society at large and Benin City in particular opened a glaring need for judicial refuge, solace and general security. There was a need for judicial redemption. There was an urgent need for deterrence to offer a minimum scare to a mob-gone-wild in the form of crime gangs operating with impunity! The Ayelala deity sprang to relevance amid this state of uncertainty and insecurity resolving land disputes and miscellaneous issues of social strife with its unconventional solutions. The oppressive party who is declared guilty in Ayelala's own judicial process, is said to suffer the typical explosive Ayelala fate. A thief in denial much like an adulterer will thus, allegedly be unmasked before the Ayelala shrine and is likely to die in abdominal explosion. Self-proclaimed eye-witnesses have reported on several informal occasions, how people were adjudicated guilty by virtue of an abdominal fate that is not subject to human manipulation or bribery.

The Ayelala movement thus grew into a formidable parallel judicial institution instilling more fear into hearts and minds than do the institutions of law enforcement and the judiciary. Such is the fear of Ayelala in Benin City that the implantation of visible symbols of this shrine on a plot of land is said to effectively scare away possible trespassers and oppressors from intrusion because they do not wish to suffer the fate of dying in abdominal explosion.

Skeptical minds however express reservations. Numerous interviews conducted with non-adherents of the "Juju" faith (as Animism is often referred to in Nigeria) paint a different picture. It must be emphasized that the numerically insignificant size of non-believers in Animism in Africa often leads to the negation of this segment of society in appraisals of this sort. Against all the odds, there are indeed, people who refuse to believe in the power of ancestors, spirits and invisible gods and simply live a rational and mundane life.

"Like its counterparts in Okija and elsewhere, Ayelala has transformed into a cult" says one legal practitioner Anslem Etuokwu – Attorney for Criminal Law and

avowed opponent of animism and the Juju faith, who I interviewed in Nigeria.

Another confidant who chose to stay anonymous also reports of widely held speculative opinions on how the process of adjudication is held before the Ayelala shrine:

"Fear has turned into followership with numerous adherents signing on to the cult. As far as I know and I stand to be corrected, people say that disputes between members of the cult and non-members are often resolved to the detriment of non-members. The non-member is given poison to drink as opposed to what the member drinks in the process of seeking Ayelala's intervention in resolving disputes before the shrine. The non-member who drinks the poison often takes ill incurably, while the member who drinks something else stays intact. If the non-member dies, it is promptly attributed to the power of the deity. The non-member may not know from the very start that his opponent is a member of the secret cult."

Today, Ayelala stands out as a contemporary example of willful notoriety. It has become instrumental to the impuned commitment of repugnant crimes of international dimension. It is today, the formidable column on which the edifice of human trafficking and international prostitution is built in the Edo State region of Nigeria.

The capital city of Edo State – Benin City – is the remnant core of ancient Benin Kingdom. It is a name that rings a bell in the ears of authentic experts of African history. For some unexplainable reasons however, Benin City has become the epicenter of export activities regarding human commodities as objects of prostitution.

Talking of Nigerian prostitutes taking over the streets of major European cities, names like Rome, Milan, Genova, etc. (all in Italy), Paris, Marseille, Lyon, etc. (all in France), Copenhagen, Oslo and diverse cities in Scandinavia as well as several cities in Germany, the Netherlands, etc. readily come to mind. Efforts to curtail this plague in several European cities have often seen law enforcement instances launching occasional clampdowns on illegal immigration and human trafficking.

My investigations revealed that law enforcement agents are aptly dismayed at the frequency with which the name "Benin City" appears as the place of birth of female illegal immigrants, prostitutes and the pimps for which the prostitutes work. The procedure has meantime, become common knowledge to the public in Benin City and the law enforcement agents of several European destinations.

At the back of it all is the desire to flee poverty and hardship in one Nigerian city that like many others, lack an industrial base and an outstanding source of gainful employment. Unlike other comparable cities however, Benin City stands out for finding a major solution to poverty and hardship in the systematic exportation of its female workforce to European cities for prostitution. This repugnant but widely embraced solution informally accepted by parents and guardians and often, by adult females has never been seriously combated with any effective government policy.

The accentuation of practical desperation could not be better underscored by the prevalent modus operandi. It all started roughly in the early 1990s. Nigerians settling in Europe sought to take advantage of the newfound boom in the domestic prostitution sector back home. Young girls were initially lured into traveling to Europe under the sponsorship of such settlers in the European continent. They were promised a better life either working as hairdressers or simply by helping their own close relatives out of domestic hardships as Nannies. There was no shortage of tricks to win the consent of the young girls. They would arrive in Europe and soon face the sober reality of having their travel documents confiscated by their sponsors and the stern order to work as prostitutes and pay back a fixed amount of money to the same sponsors. The amount to be paid would often range from $30,000 to $80,000.

In those early days, it wouldn't take the girls long to earn that much money and settle their unholy debts. The money was earned in a matter of months and the girls would start a life of their own earning more money for themselves in continued prostitution. It is like the German proverbial understanding of people who grow appetite for blood having tasted it once. Initial resistance of the urge to work as prostitutes slowly makes way for pleasure in the job and the job going viral.

These young girls returned home with enviable wealth acquiring prized properties in lavish dispositions. They became miniature celebrities and talk of the town in their localities. They became the undisputable envies of their neighborhood after making it to enviable economic heights. Having made it big, they too began to recruit their own girls and acquire more wealth and retire to family life and earn money in the comfort of their early retirement.

Soon the table turned. Instead of pimping sojourners luring young girls with dirty tricks to join the flight to Europe, today, girls openly approach sojourners begging to be taken to Europe. They declare their readiness to do all sorts of jobs the sponsors may ask them to do. Most interestingly, parents – particularly mothers – often ask their own daughters these days, to travel to Europe to do the ultimate job and uplift the family from poverty to prosperity.

Once agreed, the deal is sealed not through written contracts. Never! Sojourners who travel regularly between Europe and Nigeria choose the most effective instrument of informal adjudication. They choose adjudication before high priests, witch doctors and shrines – an instrument of fear that would send an instant chill up the spines of the diabolically intimidated local folks! These weapons of choice – deities and shrines – are overseen by self-declared witch doctors and high priests supposedly working *'for the good of mankind'*.

Ayelala being currently the most feared and dreaded of them all has today, become the favorite weapon of choice that was tailor-made in preparation for a venture that is designed to scare the hearts and minds of potential defaulters. The basic prerequisite in the current practice is of course, a meeting of minds between a sojourner and any young girl willing to travel to Europe to work as a prostitute. A large majority of such cases have the blessing of the parents. It is always a matter-of-course that the sojourner is expected to shoulder financial responsibilities that have to do with the impending travel, while parents or guardians make initial down-payments.

To safeguard the strategic interest of the sojourner, the willing young girl is brought to the Ayelala shrine before the high priest, often in the presence of her parent(s). Strands of hair are extracted from the head and the genital area alongside fingernails and toenails to serve as acceptable body parts that are used as vital objects in the ensuing occultic ritual to compel a vow of loyalty. The girl is then subjected to nudity while the animist oath is administered on her by the Ayelala high priest. She will swear to do the job for which she has been recruited, to pay back the sum of money demanded by the *'kind-hearted'* sojourner taking her out of poverty and never to betray the sojourners to the European authorities. The understanding is that failure to comply with these vows will be met with death, sudden mental illness or any other misfortune. The trick is supposedly done by the body parts extracted for the construction of the ultimate voodoo object that will remote-control the well-being of the recruited prostitute in the event of default.

Having now employed the services of the most dreadful and scary occultic deity, the sojourner proceeds with a peace of conscience to arrange all formalities involving visa, flight etc. to get the young girl overseas. In this first stage of the travel, the Ayelala cult serves as a formidable pillar for human traffickers, who successfully instill fear on their female subjects, who are criminally conveyed to Europe for prostitution or sale to other pimps who are unable to travel home on their own. Written agreements for possible litigation are effectively replaced and displaced by occultic oaths and spiritual intimidations. The ritual is not limited to Ayelala. It is also performed before other deities and shrines depending on what the beholders consider most dreadful and scary. At the present moment though, the Ayelala deity exerts the most scare on the ordinary folks of the old Benin Kingdom. Yet the sailing does not proceed smoothly or end perfectly well in all cases.

Once exposed to the daily life of prostitution in Europe, fear is quickly overtaken by the naked realities of the struggle for survival. Having traveled into Europe often using the passports of other legal residents bearing facial resemblance to the new arrival, the reality on the ground often plays out differently. The new arrival soon learns the amount of money she is expected to pay back and the earlier she got down to work the better it is for all parties involved. A suitable brothel has to be arranged for the new arrival by the sponsor, where she rents a room and pays between €100.00 and €250.00 each day depending on the attractiveness of the brothel's location. The new arrival virtually lives the life of an outlaw in the real sense of the word, in a European society that is in contrast to Nigeria's disorderly society, far better organized. It is a life underground using the identity documents of a look-alike compatriot! Initial problems begin however when the new arrival takes ill. Without health insurance that is mandatory and common in a typical European society, treatment is obtained using the borrowed identity of a look-alike, who definitely has a different medical history. The severity of the circumstances is even exacerbated when the new arrival experiences her first menstrual period while working in the brothel. Her boss will waste no time frowning and making her understand that such impediments to earnings are undesirable irrespective of her helplessness. This comes on top of other stressful peripheral conditions.

Changing economic conditions across several European countries have long translated into severe difficulties in raising the amount of money expected to be paid to the sponsors of the travel into Europe or any other pimp who may have bought over the new arrival from the sponsors of the travel. Occasional police raids on brothels to fish out illegal residents sometimes translate into the arrest and threatened deportation of such new arrivals. This makes the sight of police officers the greatest scare for such new arrivals.

In years gone by when the African pimping phenomenon was yet on a low profile, thousands of Dollars were earned very quickly in a matter of months. Police scare was at its lowest and black prostitutes were just something new and desirable to Johns and Punters. My investigations uncovered that new arrivals at the time, often paid up within three to six months and then had time to take care of themselves and sort out their own residential status. They would find a European man to marry and take them out of the awry world of prostitution; such marriages would legalize their stay while they themselves graduated into the next level of becoming sponsors and pimps.

Today, patronage of black prostitutes is reserved almost exclusively for those who love and admire the black female with the urge to date and have a taste of carnal knowledge outside their own race. This brings us face to face with another problem of racism in the profession. The new arrival is confronted head-on with a new problem that she has never known or anticipated all her life. She begins to learn all of a sudden, that her skin color makes a difference in the performance of her job. It makes her supposedly inferior to her white counterparts in terms of customers' preference. In extreme cases, this minority status keeps African prostitutes reaping one patronizing customer for almost every five, six or up to ten customers patronizing a white counterpart.

Asian prostitutes from countries such as Thailand and those from Eastern Europe, who are widely regarded as having a better mastery of the horizontal game and business, enjoy far better patronage. Faced with all these emerging and meanwhile, consolidated routine difficulties, I discovered in the course of my investigations that the black African prostitute was and still is increasingly confronted with the existential problem of sometimes, not being able to pay the fee demanded by sponsors and pimps often after several years of working in the sex business.

The psychological dilemma of realizing how much material sacrifices were made by their respective parents back home for initial down-payment to the sponsors and pimps serves to exacerbate the pains and frustration suffered by such sex workers on the ground. Calling home to explain the difficulties to parents or guardians, they will often be reminded in the most polite language, of the spiritual, occultic and sometimes physical consequences of not keeping their own sides of the bargain. Aside the enduring fear of facing the wrath of the Ayelala or other deities, parents and siblings may sometimes be subjected to the risk of criminal intimidations and physical assaults by sponsors or their cronies.

In extreme cases which are now becoming commonplace, the frustrations grow. I discovered that such girls are even unable to pay the daily rent of their rooms in brothels. The priority of feeding and taking care of themselves grows increasingly difficult. Sending money home to assist their own family becomes very difficult and almost impossible. In the aftermath, they take the ultimate decision of disappearing and going even farther underground to escape their sponsors and pimps suffering a double jeopardy in seeking to escape the detection of their illegal status by the police and now, on the run also from their sponsors and pimps. Escaping sponsors and pimps intrinsically requires that the young girls are no longer giving a damn about the Ayelala oath and the consequences of criminal intimidations of and physical assaults on their parents back home. They escape their predators often with the knowledge that their parents may suffer dire consequences.

At this point, the sponsors and pimps revert to Ayelala again. They will have the cult summon the parents and wards of the fleeing prostitute. These days, such summoning is even done in the most formal manner possible. The Chief Priest of the Ayelala shrine issues an official letter summoning the family member or representative of the prostitute, who were parties to the initial oath swearing that saw the successful smuggling abroad of the prostitute. If the initial oath was not taken before the Ayelala shrine, the complaining party then provides the identity and address of the defendant to be summoned by the shrine's high priest. Ayelala will then reiterate its formidable strength by reminding the summoned subjects of the lethal power it commands over human life. This is then followed by a serious search for a workable compromise in the course of oral hearings before the high priest. Under the fear of death and perceived evil influences of spirits and gods, the parents or representatives of the fleeing prostitute are often forced to come clean and explain the difficulties encountered by the subject. In the final analysis, a solution is worked out backed by the clout of Ayelala's domineering power over life and death.

The most common solution that is suggested – according to my investigations – is to get the fleeing subject to commit to the payment of a monthly installment through the parents or wards leading the diabolical proceedings before the Ayelala shrine. The money is paid directly to the High Priest of the shrine through wire transfer. The sponsor or pimp or any of its delegated representatives collects the money from the shrine. Whatever amount is agreed (often beginning from €300.00), one hundred Euros is basically reserved for the Ayelala high priest as his own commission for the spiritual services, in every single month of the installment payment. Today, there are a countless number of such cases illegally handled and adjudicated by the Ayelala high priest. The process secures the longer term recovery of the money to which sponsors and pimps lay claim as well as buoys up the financial clout of the Ayelala movement given the value of a €100.00 collected each month and on multiple basis depending on the number of cases adjudicated. It should be borne in mind that €100.00 has a local value almost as high as €1,000.00 in Europe.

In this pervasive psyche of fear and submission to unknown powers, the immense supportive role of the Ayelala cult in the perpetration of pimping and smuggling of young girls out of Nigeria cannot be over-emphasized. Being the currently most feared of them all, Ayelala is today, the citadel and most formidable deitetic force behind which the industry of exploitation of young girls hides in Benin City.

In a society, in which even criminals believe in the powers of deities and spirits to protect them from falling into the hands of law enforcement and judicial authorities, I will not be surprised if claims are also advanced, of further nefarious involvements of the Ayelala movement in the perpetration of other sorts of domestic crimes. After all, it is not unusual to read reports of ritual killings and the related reports of witch doctors offering protective amulets, talismans and other forms of 'invoked forces' to protect robbers, kidnappers and murderers from death. Some even believe to have their skins well prepared by witch doctors, from bullet penetration – some concocted bulletproof skin of sort. On September 02, 2012, the Nigerian Vanguard carried the headline news: *"Man shoots son dead in failed 'bulletproof' charm test"*! The man identified as Ornguga Adega of Agbatse village in the Kwande local government area of Benue State shot his only (ten-year-old) son dead. He had bought the bulletproof charm-cream from a witch doctor, which he rubbed on the young boy's body before performing the fatal experiment.[51] This is not an isolated case in Africa except that many will not have the courage to perform the experiment by themselves.

It will not come as a surprise if information emerges today, also pointing to the role of Ayelala biting off its own share of the proceeds of crime in this lethal sector.

Reverence for deities and spirits represented by shrines has long been a natural part of Black Africa's DNA. They are known in different forms dating back to the very early times of tribal life. In times, in which common phenomena of life were perceived as awry and subjected to wild interpretations, every phenomenon was regarded as being the manifestation of an underlying god. The god of iron (Ogun) according to oral reports, is today, therefore believed to be responsible for vehicle, airplane or naval accidents, wars, etc. while the god of thunder (Shango) may be held accountable for natural disasters, thunder and lightning being the physical expression of the intensity of the wrath of the gods. Thunder and lightning are thus often regarded as heralding impending interventions of the gods with the varying intensities of such intervention being subjected to interpretation by priests and witch doctors depending on attendant elements such as the whirlwind, frequency of lightning and the decibel strength of projected thunder. On the contrary, the god of the water world (Olokun) is largely associated with peace and protection. The list could go on endlessly.

As in the Brazilian example of "Umbanda, Quimbanda and Candomble", shrines and high priests in Africa are thus representatives of individual deities. The type of deity consulted or patronized thus depends on the worries of the individual seeking the protection of the gods as well as the nature of protection or curative assistance desired. In search of protection from road accidents or death by the bullet of a gun, a client is most likely to employ the services of an Ogun (god of iron) high priest. Most often, a Priest would foresee unexpected events in the course of consultancies. The gods will have to be quickly appeased with sacrifices to forestall misfortunes such as accidents or the impending attack of witches of the underworld. Herein lies the suspicion of fraud by rational analysts and observers. After all the visions seen by witch doctors and self-proclaimed sorcerers can never be subjected to objective proofs or verification.

Social Behavior guided by spiritism

Deriving from the awesomeness and implied as well as accepted larger-than-life powers of the various deities and the spirits of deceased relatives, individuals regulate their general social behavior in a manner that will prevent them from inviting the wrath of deities and spirits upon themselves. Taboos, abominations, prohibitions and generally deprecated social behaviors and behavioral guidelines are thus shaped largely in line with the understanding that the powers of unseen deities and spirits are limitless and pervasive.

In many spheres of life, social taboos and abominations in Africa are not different from same in many other parts of the world. In some cases, the logical explanations underlying such taboos differ sharply. In Africa, such explanations in some cases may even serve to stupefy the folks further than the emptiness of such taboos.

In one example, we will attempt to show here, how Black African communities regard and handle the behavior of women after the death of their husbands. They do not take kindly to a woman re-marrying too quickly after the death of her husband. Depending on the society and the region in Africa, tradition may demand of such women to mourn the death of their husbands and indulge in abstinence for a period that may range from six months to as much as seven years. On the contrary, almost no notice whatsoever is taken of a man who chooses to remarry after the death of his wife. Condolence and grief at the loss of such a wife, is often accompanied by the expression of understanding for the urgent need to get a new wife to keep the household moving.

Indeed my experience in Europe has shown that a similar situation in which a spouse re-marries too quickly after the death of the partner is also not often greeted with applause. The difference conversely, is that the European expects a spouse to show signs of sorrow in a manner that would not make the death appear like good riddance to bad rubbish. The European has no gender differentiation in such cases. I remember the case of the former ceremonial President of Germany Roman Herzog, whose wife died aged 63. In announcing his readiness to re-marry another 60-year old lady, the 67-year old President Herzog made it abundantly clear in the year 2001 that he had to wait for the expiration of the unwritten one-year mourning period to announce his new love. Of course, people murmured and insinuated a long-standing romance before the expiration of the pseudo-obligatory mourning period. There was a general frown at the obviously unintended impression of 'good riddance' to a marriage of 42 years.

In Africa however, traditional beliefs have been passed down from several generations unchanged. While the female spouse, who is on the receiving end, is clearly discriminated against, she is also served the fairy tale of inviting the wrath of the spirit of the departed husband if she fails to mourn him in a befitting manner. Any fate suffered by a bereaved wife within the imposed period of mourning will therefore be promptly characterized as the handiwork of the furious spirit of the dead husband. One conspicuous example is the case of infant mortality that is rampant in Africa. Should the bereaved wife lose any child after the period of re-marrying, the reason is readily made out. It does and will not matter at all that infant mortality is a huge problem that the continent has been grappling with over several decades.

In some traditions however, specific gods and not the spirit of the departed husband are conceived as forces behind the declared misfortune of premature re-marrying. The rituals and ceremonies that are consequentially imposed on a bereaved wife to appease the gods or the spirits of the departed ones either to forestall the occurrence of any misfortune or halt the rampaging impact of spiritual anger ends up these days, enriching witch doctors. Such witch doctors in their self-proclaimed power of clairvoyance routinely present themselves as mediums linking the living with the dead and the gods of the land. They do not only charge money for their services in performing the 'necessary' rituals and ceremonies, the cost of getting the materials (cowries, coins, feathers and other petty objects, live animals often goats, sheep, fowls, etc.) demanded for such processes often end up taking a toll on the financial strength of the subject person.

Another example of social behavior guided by spiritual explanation is incestuous relationships. While there is a near global consensus on the biological and genetic inadequacies of incestuous practices, several African societies discourage incestuous practices by advancing the anger of the gods and spirits of all sorts. Today, given a scientifically established high risk of adverse health consequences in the chain of incestuous multiplication, the act is highly stigmatized and in many cases, prohibited by law in some countries of the world. In Africa however, the prohibitive factor is lesser the law than the fear of the wrath of spirits and gods.

I remember a case of a young lady who, for reasons ranging from psychological to environmental constraints suffered insomnia. Compatible with scientific findings, a few days of serial sleeplessness finally took its toll on the lady's nerves and mental health. Total nervous breakdown was followed by symptoms of hallucination. Incompetent and unqualified medical services failed to identify her problems or prescribe simple sleeping aid or tranquilizers during exhaustive efforts within the limits of her financial capacity. Subsequent to a steadily worsening condition aggravated by bad dreams, nightmares and daydreaming, the last option was the services of witch doctors and spiritualists. She was promptly diagnosed with keeping a strong secret within her for which she was being punished by the spirits and the gods. Relentless pressure to have her reveal her secret uncovered the story of an incestuous relationship that she had supposedly had with her elder brother. The state of mind surrounding such purported 'confession' failed to play a role in questioning the veracity. Euphoria and the arousing impact of sensationalism cemented the urge to sustain the absolute veracity of what would normally have gone down as a dubious confession. Sanctions ranging from mere admonishments through stigmatization up until an aggressive confrontation of the suspected elder brother were potential reactions that trailed this absolute taboo of intra-family sexual intercourse. It promptly became a family headline news-item. Urgent measures had to be taken to appease the gods. In the lady's case, the spirit of her dead father was 'seen' to be tormenting her. Pastors prayed for 'deliverance' while witch doctors performed rituals and sacrifices. Sacrifices included the slaughtering of a goat and other livestock to appease the alleged rampaging forces of the gods and the spirits!

Was no one enlightened enough in this family saga, to weigh the logical sequences of the incident? Aside the fact that the dubious confession made under a state of nervous and mental breakdown should have been taken with a pinch of salt, the scientific reality that incest – detestable and sickly as it is – is never a reason for mental and nervous breakdown was kept completely off the radar of logical considerations in a characteristic African manner. Even if anyone thought of it, he/she would not have dared to voice it out as the belief was so strongly embedded in the general psyche. The plight of the young lady whose failing state of mental health was treated with the power of the spirits and the gods will never be known, but the general state of African belief system remains intact as much as its impact on the physical, social and mental development of the entire continent.

The impact of collective stupefaction and dumbness through generations is yet not a political program deemed necessary by politicians to be confronted aggressively within the scope of public education. As in several other areas of burning public issues that should be at the center of public education, public awareness of the genetic impact of incestuous reproduction is still at its lowest possible level. The fear of gods and spirits makes people easier to control by powers and stakeholders having enough to gain from the persistence of traditional institutions. Witch doctors are enriched and grow from strength to strength in their grip on general sub-consciousness while the unsuspecting folks remain ignorant in perpetual mental darkness.

* * * * *

Chapter 4

Traditional Monarchies and the concept of god-kings!

Aside witch doctors and self-proclaimed sorcerers, one of the strongest powers that stand to gain from the persistence of traditional orders in Sub-Saharan Africa is the institution of traditional monarchies spread across different societies.

Ancient Africa thrived on kingdoms of various sizes. Wars of territorial expansion made some kingdoms larger and more significant than the others. These kingdoms – big or small – however had one feature in common: the reverence for kings! Monarchs were usually regarded as god-kings. Post-colonial western-style governmental structures that have grown stronger into our present day have seen the steady decline of the powers and influences of these god-kings.

Indeed colonial explorers of the ancient British Empire took its time to observe the influence of traditional monarchs when they first stepped on African soil creating colonies and reaping economic benefits through exploitations. It did not take the British long at the time, to understand the emptiness of public awe and reverence that indigenous folks had for the tribal monarchs.

The ancient Benin Kingdom in present-day Nigeria was one example of such nations that accepted collective fear of monarchical powers as a normal way of life much like several other traditional empires and monarchies in the continent. The tribal monarchy of the Benin Kingdom was one that impressed the British observers with the organized nature of its governmental structure which bore much similarity to what the British knew from home. The monarch as head of government had a cabinet comprising minister-like cronies who oiled the government's machinery in the active function of effecting the division of administrative labor. The Ministers bore different titles that could be easily equated with the designations known in western governmental structures. There was however this distinctive demarcation that the ministers were generally regarded as not being 'ordinary humans'. In fact, one of the 'ministerial' portfolios was responsible for overseeing witchcraft and the activities of the spirits and gods. A job-description for an ordained head of witches so to speak! In the overall equation, the monarch himself stood out as the super-ordinate instance and an Alfa and Omega over supernatural powers!

The concept of god-king is however not limited to Africa. The King of Tibet – the *Dalai Lama* – is also a god-king slightly similar to god-kings as understood by Africans. From the point of view of reverence and the local value accorded by the Tibetan folks to their god-king, authentic similarities can be identified in status comparison. That may however, be the point where such similarities end. Without going into details on the structure of the Tibetan monarchy though, it may suffice to state at this juncture that the process of choosing the Tibetan Monarch-for-life is based on the localized Tibetan Buddhist principles of identifying reincarnation relationships. This today, is the central legacy that makes the Tibetan King what he is.[52] In many African tribes though, the monarch is not chosen but inherited.

It is undeniably, an inevitable task in Tibet, to identify and proclaim whose reincarnation the King is as well as understand the quality of selfless service to humanity that this precise reincarnation portends. In other words, the mission of the Tibetan King has to be such that is accepted as super and extra-ordinary. The king will be in a position to master all the demands of Buddhist practices from meditation, teachings, astral travel, upholding moral values to living as a shining example for his folks. Like the routine master of any Buddhist temple, monastery and community as seen in any Asian country, the

Dalai Lama thus stands out as a Grandmaster of the entire Tibetan Buddhist folks. The Dalai Lama knows no witchcraft and does not fight evil forces but seeks to guide his folks towards strengthening the power of positive elevation of humanity. The guiding principle being: "Where positive energy thrives, there can be no evil forces." Today's 14th Dalai Lama of Tibet – the monk *Tendzin Gyatsho* – never gets weary explaining wherever he can and to anyone who cares to listen, that he is nothing but a simple Buddhist monk. He emphasizes that he has no power over anything more than any other person has.[(52)]

On the contrary, god-Kings in Africa live and thrive on the understanding that they are super-human. They would prefer their folks to believe that they command powers to watch over life and death and clearly negate the fact that they too die like everyone else! They encourage popular belief in the notion that they command powers over the good and the evil and are super witches, wizards, sorcerers in the super-ordinate instance. News about their general state of health never filters through to public square. Nothing is ever heard of them falling occasionally ill like everyone of their subjects. They are generally perceived as infallible and are as a consequence, the Grandmaster of witches.

Careful observation and understanding of the functional mechanism of ancient Benin Kingdom's governmental institution convinced the British colonial adventurers to adopt a system of indirect rule.

Without the ordinary folks noticing their presence, British interventionists would first inundate the monarch with valuable gifts including guns and gun powder to endow him with a sense of armament superiority in a region that was characterized by wars of territorial expansion. Very soon however, they would move to convert the monarch into a remote-controlled puppet that was configured to take instructions on how to rule his people on matters affecting British interests. When one such god-King in the Benin Kingdom *Oba Ovonramwen* proved stubborn to be dictated to, he was banished from his own territorial kingdom without much ado and subjected to solitary incarceration in far-away Calabar – a city that bubbled with colonial activities. The same city that witnessed Mary Slessor's historical feat in her fight for the abolition of the killing of twins! In his spirit of defiance and resistance, oral history reports that Oba Ovonramwen of the Benin Kingdom embarked on a hunger strike. A hunger strike that reportedly lasted close to one-month!

Till today, the length of time of this hunger strike is attributed by the Binis to a piece of tiny cloth (*Ukugba*), which the King reportedly tied around his waist like a belt. Tightening this 'magical' belt each passing day, meant that the king was able to kill the feeling of hunger and thus able to survive and sustain hunger-striking for the length of time that he did without eating any meal. This length of time being generally accepted by the Binis as impossible to endure by any 'normal' human being!

Today however, the leader of the defunct Irish Republican Army (IRA) and member of the British Parliament – *Bobby Sands* – who died on May 05, 1981 hunger-striking in protest of the British occupation of Ireland has put a lie to this claim. Bobby Sands' own hunger strike lasted 66 days[53] about one month in excess of Oba Ovonramwen's reported one-month strike. Bobby Sands ate no food and tied no magical belt.

The monarch of the Benin Kingdom would have been reduced to the status of an ordinary person if there was no super-ordinary tale to explain his survival without food for a length of time that people must understand, was impossible for a normal human being.

The value of the Oba of Benin that is characterized by reverence, adoration and high esteem, which are not based on any specific personal achievement for humanity or society, is an endemic characteristic of African societies. We say this in this discourse, without prejudice to the functional benefits that this position holds for general social and political life.

This was clearly underscored lately by a daring act of the current Benin monarch (now filling a monumental historical gap in a modern world of rational leadership that de-emphasizes the relevance of deities) that finally turned out to be an embarrassment than a benefit.

For the avoidance of doubt, it must be underscored at this juncture that the purpose of this exposé on the monarchy and god-Kings in Africa aims exclusively at highlighting the folly of wrong beliefs and its impact on Africa's under-developed status and not to disparage the entities and holders of the revered positions. Without doubt, the current Oba of Benin even stands out as highly respectable in view of his exploitation of the very limited powers available to him, to impact on good governance through constructive critiquing relying on the respect accorded him and his words and thus, the value of his utterances.

Nonetheless, his very well-meaning attempt to contribute in his own little way, to the curbing and eradication of the rising and menacing wave of murder, kidnapping and robbery within the core of the territory that his forefathers once ruled over ended up in an image disaster.

In an obvious attempt to offer moral support to the failed system of law enforcement and justice, the king of the ancient kingdom resorted to a weapon that would have sent a chill up the spine of the individual folk in the 16th century. The king's palace resolved to cast a spiritual spell in public, on the perpetrators and executors of all the violent crimes that made life unbearable for the common man. The palace summoned the 'superior forces' of the supernatural world within its fold and brought them to the gaze of the public. In ceremonies and rituals that would have once created unspeakable fright and awe in the eyes and mind of the beholders, spells were declared cast on kidnappers, robbers, assassins and all perpetrators of violent crimes, their facilitators, benefactors and all forms of associates. They were to be visited by death and calamitous afflictions if they continued their evil deeds. Initially, it seemed to have worked. For a few days in the aftermath of the public curse, there was calm within the core territory of the ancient Benin Kingdom. Analysts kept a close look at further development to see if the model would qualify for nationwide adoption to backup the law enforcement process. Media houses began to report on people who had hitherto remained unknown as criminals, suddenly thronging to the palace begging to have the spells on them unraveled. The fear that gripped such people was the fear of the unknown. Since any misfortune that may occur in the aftermath of casting the public spell would be easily attributed to the spell itself, redemption was seen in repentance and quiet appeal to the monarch to unravel the spell from them personally.

Within a week or two though, there was a dramatic twist. As if in sudden realization that the spells were mere spoken words that should not hinder them from their dubious source of illegal earnings, crime rate suddenly soared again to its previous level. Some attributed this to non-indigenes who did not know the value and immense consequences of spells cast by the king and therefore inundated the territory with imported crimes. Even if this unproven assertion was true though, indigenous criminals may have simply observed that the royal spell did not have any short or medium-term impact even on those importers of the prevailing crime. They joined the fold and crime rate soared all the more. In the end, it was the image and reputation of the king that suffered a serious dent that no one loved or had the courage to speak about.

Even though modern systems of governance – from dictatorships to constitutional democracies – have largely ensured the complete political insignificance of traditional monarchies in our present day Africa, the peasant folk with the lowest level of school education continue to hold on to the traditional values of the institution. With the exception of the Kingdoms of Lesotho and Swaziland where constitutional and absolute monarchies are practiced[54], the institution of kings, chiefs and royal titles that came into our modern days as relics of pre-colonial history are meticulously preserved only as traditional and cultural heritages. Operatives and forces driving the engines of these institutions however are anything but pleased about their own disempowerment. To salvage anything left of political relevance, they foster a continuing process of highlighting and keeping alive, those perceived supernatural attributes that made them relevant to their folks through history. The least educated ones in society as well as some educated adherents and irrational Pan-Africanist fanatics who seek to sell the undifferentiated idea of the superiority of the African identity are the primary addressees and recipients of such campaigns. The end-result of mass stupefaction seeing Africa ever lagging behind the rest of the world in education and all facets of social and industrial development is never recognized as one by-product of the influence of this pervasive belief in supernatural forces. It should be emphasized however that there is no single proof of an overall inferiority of the African traditional way of life in general to any foreign lifestyle. Indicative scientific assumptions do not offer any evidence however, to show that the irrational attachment to a lifestyle built on the fear of the unknown encouraged by specific traditional interest groups can ever serve as a strong promotional factor of social and political development.

Indeed, it is one thing to decry and condemn the crimes and evils of colonialism and the unbalanced nature of modern economic and political imperialism. It is another issue altogether, to contend that such contents of the African socio-political life as the colonialists had sought to discourage under the label of "primitivity" are indeed superior to their alternatives simply because our ancestors lived with them successfully. In a changing world with new industrial and environmental challenges however, the days of pure *Herbalism* and *Spiritist* misconceptions are clearly days confined to history. We live in a world of science and technology that Africa is yet to fully wake up to.

* * * * *

Chapter 5

Explorative Science:
Not in the African DNA?

Sometime in 1979, I attended a musical concert in a sports stadium in Nigeria. The performer was Nigeria's superstar of blessed memory Fela Anikulapo Kuti. He was duetting with the American star Roy Ayers. It was a concert, in which I had the rare privilege of taking a personal photo with the Afrobeat king on stage shortly after the show. I felt like I had won a jackpot and kept this photo in a strategically conspicuous position in my room to boost my childish ego as a blossoming teenager until the Polaroid photo wore out with time. Indeed, the day I took this photo was to be the last time I saw Fela Anikulapo Kuti alive.

Since gaining nationwide fame, Fela Kuti has always answered to the family name that Nigerians and his fans worldwide knew to be Ransome-Kuti.

His siblings including the renowned Professor of medicine Beko also used the last name Ransome-Kuti and Fela bore this name for several years.

To underscore his love for the black continent and what it represents (positives and negatives) Fela became the only member of his family to do away with the word "Ransome" which he termed western and a colonial heritage. In his convictions and actions, Fela was pan-Africanist to the core. He would prefer treating illnesses using African herbal combinations to any Aspirin or Paracetamol and preach same in his muisical concerts. *"After all our ancestors used such herbal combinations successfully for several centuries, before the imperialists intervened to pollute our unison with nature"* Fela would literally tell his audience while lecturing them in the local version of the English language that is interlaced with the regional dialect – the "Pidgin English".

Fascinated as I was by this argument at the time, my teenage exuberance did not endow me with the wisdom to ask intelligent questions. For instance I failed in the intellectual duty to ask if there were statistical records of death and survival rates to verify the efficacy of those herbal combinations that our ancestors survived on. I also failed to ask if the rate of infant mortality in Africa in the days of our ancestors was different from or better than what we have been experiencing since the death of colonialism. But I knew for sure that our ancestors often explained deaths as the wrath of one god or the other or the evil deeds of some sinister witches and sorcerers, but hardly ever as a natural occurrence unless it happens to a King who is involuntarily considered as superseding all witches and evil forces. Then it was simply the king's time to return to his ancestors.

Within the period in which I watched Fela Anikulapo Kuti on stage in a stadium, his change of name from "Ransome" to "Anikulapo" was yet a fresh issue in headline news overtaken only by the climax of his incessant conflict with the military government of Nigeria at the time. The climax of his conflict with political authority, was of course, the burning down of his house – the "Kalakuta Republic" that was also impounded on orders from the military government of the time.

During the musical concert in the soccer stadium, Fela Kuti had a special message for his audience. In every concert, Fela Anikulapo Kuti reserved time for what he called "Yabis!" In the context of Nigerian Pidgin English, the word "Yabis" is the substantive of the Pidgin English verb "to yab" taken from the original English word "yap!" In the Pidgin English context however, "yabbing" means scolding and satirical critiquing. When yapping begins, Fela would fearlessly take on all the powerful men of society one after the other exposing their crimes and weaknesses in rhetorical sophistication and often in unquestionable logical sequences. No wonder, he earned himself the reputation of going in and out of prison at regular intervals. Aside the love for the music of Fela Anikulapo Kuti though, the yapping session in his concerts was always the highlight and climax of his shows that people waited relentlessly to share. It was the time, in which public education the *Kuti-style* takes center stage and everyone learns something new about the society and takes something home to ponder upon.

Fela's subject during this precise concert was the crimes of colonialism and the systematic misrepresentation of historical facts by the colonial Europeans and their perverted version of historical truths about Africa. Fela talked about the River Niger and questioned the veracity of claims that every pupil learned in Primary School's history classes. Teachers taught us in those days that the Scottish explorer Mungo Park who died in 1806[55] actually discovered the source of the Niger River. During yapping time in this concert, Fela told us of accounts in history books that narrated Mungo Park's interactions with the local folks in the course of his expedition on the Niger River. The local folks had shown him which way to proceed to lead him forward in his Niger River course. Since the local folks had no system of scientific documentation however, Mungo Park went down in the colonialists own version of history, as the discoverer of the source of the Niger River. Since a lot of African peasant folks lived with, along and around this river even before the coming of the Whiteman, this claim in history, of Mungo Park being the discoverer of the source of River Niger could not have been true, Fela told us loud and clear. The thundering applause that greeted this comment signaled the general approval of his audience.

In today's world of online encyclopedia however, Wikipedia reports that Mungo Park was only the first European to encounter the Niger River. Even though we did not look for other sources to support or contradict Wikipedia's account of Mungo Park's expedition for the purpose of this discourse, Wikipedia definitely does not mention in any passage that Mungo Park discovered the source of the Niger River. As a living witness though, I can confirm Fela Anikulapo Kuti's representation of claims in history that this Scottish man was the discoverer of River Niger's source. Our Nigerian teachers taught us this fact very clearly in primary schools and these teachers were not cooking up stories. They also, probably learnt this fact from model syllabuses and curriculums left behind by the colonialists who founded and shaped the educational system left behind in their former colonies.

Be that as it may though, our purpose in this discourse has a different focus altogether. It does not matter to us one bit in this discourse if Mungo Park discovered the source of the River Niger or not. What matters to us is the lesson to be drawn from the expedition undertaken by Mungo Park and other Europeans like him.

In seeking to understand and identify reasons for Africa's failure to move forward even in the face of changing or in some cases, conducive social and environmental conditions, the pervasive emphasis on supernatural powers in African life will always stand out as one undisputable factor. History books tell us today about outstanding explorative feats attributable to people like Vasco da Gama of Spain who reportedly discovered the sea route to India and Christopher Columbus of Italy who uncovered the Americas to European curiosity. Today, we hear of Reinhold Messner an Austrian adventurer, who made name in recent times overcoming one mountain height after the other including the Everest, trying to dare the Arctic and embarking on several adventures and carrying out scientific experiments. There are countless names of Europeans simply testing the limits of human abilities swimming across the channel between England and France, and other nationals swimming from Cuba to the United States, etc.

Indeed, records show that the adventure embarked upon by Vasco da Gama to discover the sea route to India was predicated by several attempts by people who either perished in dangerous weather conditions at sea or in the hands of pirates. Vessels constructed for expeditions in those early centuries were of course, nothing more than instruments of involuntary suicide judging by today's standards. Yet the death or disappearance of one adventurer is sooner or later followed by another adventurer with some slightly improved instrument of facilitation. This is true of Mungo Park, it is true of Christopher Columbus and even true of today's Reinhold Messner and other daring climbers and swimmers.

Now, for some unexplainable reasons however, the DNA of the black African seemed configured to face environmental challenges with a different mindset altogether. While the Europeans were busy probing into the mystery of life and the universe by coming up with one verifiable scientific fact after the other and achieving feats after feats for the common good and benefit of the whole of humanity, the black African was busy identifying different gods and spirits to explain those phenomena that he could not understand. While the European was daring mysterious ocean waves, the vicious and intimidating lightning and the accompanying rain, the black African was seeing the anger of the gods behind the vicious waves and the tears of the spirits in the downpour of rain and simply took to worshipping these unexplainable phenomena.

In the African context though, the loss of lives – not one or two but several lives – in the attempt to sail to India and discover a sea route, would have long been interpreted without much ado, as an impossible task. A task that some god or spirit may have put a jinx upon! Weird and wild stories would have been invented by self-imposed clairvoyant witch doctors communicating with the spirits and gods of the sea. Such stories would have made the round to the ordinary folks and instilled fear on them to avoid the sea as the region of guaranteed death. One after the other however, the European embarked on this deadly project and brought it to a logical conclusion. Today, mankind is better off for it.

It therefore comes as no surprise that a European comes to Africa from nowhere and tells the folks that he has discovered the source of a river that was long known to the local residents. Indeed, what would the source of a river matter to an African of those days when it can be considered as the mysterious meeting point of witches in the dead of night? In fact, I will not be surprised if any African who overcame the rivers in those early days and was able to swim, got recorded in history as having been in possession of supernatural powers.

In other words, neither the rivers, oceans nor the mountains meant anything to the African nor did the source of any irrelevant River Niger have any scientific significance to him. Indeed it will be no surprise if in the present day there are still a vast number of people in the African continent believing in the awesomeness and supernatural sanctity of such a source of a mighty mysterious river.

Having also passed through this process of basic and elementary human instincts of spontaneous reverence for unknown phenomena, the European thought he could understand where Africa stood and sought to transform the African completely. The European then sought to discourage the African from idol worshipping or the worshipping of phenomena simply because he was unable to understand the underlying complexity.

The European thus began to teach the African to embrace Christianity and the concept of Jesus Christ as the only savior and source of redemption. The African was then taught to do away with the filth and stink of decaying blood and bones placed on the shrines of worshipped idols. It was to be replaced by the immaculate whiteness of the churches altar and preacher's pulpit. The underlying principle was however the same. The concept of a supernatural being and one Alpha and Omega who had the key to life in his hands! An invisible force that had to be worshipped and adored in faith and trust without questions and logical probes!

This was however diametrically opposed to the scientific zeitgeist of explorers and researchers who dared all beliefs and fears to achieve rational goals and unravel the mysteries of life in several areas seeking to free the mind from phenomena that were generally thought mystical and mysterious.

These confusing and incompatible signals sent by the European colonialists of advancing education and science alongside religion and the blind belief in God and Jesus Christ then made several enlightened Africans to question the notion of declaring the African ways inferior. After all, the bottom line was nothing more than belief in deities and forces unknown to man be they God, Jesus Christ or the god of thunder. In the end, the African convinced himself that his religious ways of worshipping several gods and spirits could not have been so wrong after all. They also believed in the one and super-ordinate God above all else! The ancestors survived on them for several centuries and social order remained well organized for the prevailing circumstances of the time.

The coexistence of science and religion with science gaining the upper hand in terms of bringing palpable relief to the daily life of mankind and religion only playing the function of maintaining social and moral values requiring prayers for abstract heavenly achievements did not seem to convince anyone that the African religions were inferior. More so, the reality that the residual identity of the Christian religion in advanced western societies these days hardly differs from what the world knows as upholding moral values and a sense of humaneness seems to bolster this general perception. It is also one clear reality that is held high in the outward projection of the Christian faith.

In the end, Africa accepted Christianity, Science and the European system of government that has no place for traditional rulers. Alongside these, Africa also kept its monarchs, belief systems, institutions and cultural identity. In the final analysis, the prevailing picture is one of a confused continent that simply does not really seem to understand what to do with the dialectics of scientific and religious contradictions.

Today, they hear the veteran scientist quoted in the early pages of this work Prof. Stephen Hawking saying *"there is no need for a Creator to explain the existence of the universe."* Then the bible talks of sacrilege in questioning the supremacy of God as the creator of living beings.

While academic education has taken a solid hold and found its place in every African society, scientific exploration and researches have yet failed to take any hold whatsoever on any region of the continent (discounting South Africa and its Apartheid era success in researches in heart transplant made by the Afrikaner Dr. Chris Barnard). Today, hardly any meaningful science is practiced in institutions of higher learning in Sub-Saharan Africa beyond the blabbering of theoretical quips that are scarcely bolstered by practical laboratory experimentation to say the least of implementation. Experts attribute this partly to the availability of fewer resources as well as the clear shortage of know-how and the will to commit to altruism.

The selfless demands of commitment to scientific research at a lower level can hardly thrive in a society dominated by a public psyche of seeking to get rich overnight. Selfless commitment to scientific research in this sense would simply constitute a waste of time in the reasoning of those responsible. A Minister would thus prefer a diversion of budgetary allocations for universities into his own pocket rather than dreaming of the feats and glory that will be his and his country's upon breaking grounds in scientific research. The same applies to the Dean of Faculty, Head of Department and the Professor at the lowest segment of the ladder of responsibility.

While the question remains unanswered if a large section of African professors are even knowledgeable enough to guide their students in sophisticated scientific research works, we will simply assume for the purpose of this discourse that they are. Yet the continent is inundated with such academic leaders as would rather divert funds into their own pockets, even whenever the money managed to trickle down their way.

One laughable example is the Nigerian Institute of Oil Palm Research (NIFOR) that was founded in 1939 during the colonial days. Parts of its objectives were *"To do research on Nigerian Palm, Biotechnology, Plant Production & Protection, Socioeconomic & Farming Systems, Food Processing and..."*[56] bla, bla, bla!

Indigenous Nigerians today, ridicule just one reality mocking the existence of this institute. The reality contends that Indonesians or Malaysians (whichever of the two countries does not really seem to matter) once sent scholars to this institute very many years ago. Their mission was to learn the process of extracting oil from palm kernels. They came, they saw, they learned and returned home. I will hasten to add here though that this claim of Indonesians or Malaysians coming to Nigeria to learn the extraction of palm oil even though an unverified fact that I as a writer, cannot vouch for, the veracity or not matters very little against the backdrop of the comparative progression that Nigeria has witnessed when weighed against these two countries. Yet, there is a serious lesson to be learnt from the gist if we assume the story to be true.

Today, Indonesia or Malaysia have now advanced the utilization of palm oil to the level of creating Diesel out of palm oil in the search for a substitute for petroleum oil. The Nigerian Institute of Oil Palm Research has however advanced steadily. Not in scientific research but in backward research witnessing dilapidation and retrogression! It has lived through years of successive leadership expertise in the art of stealing budgetary allocations. Not a single scientific ground has been broken. Not even in the art of cracking individual palm nuts or coconuts! All since the year 1939!

Science in Africa is as good as non-existent. The Nigerian example shows that African universities are today inundated with cultism, rituals and practices that are incompatible with scientific teachings. Not only are students involved in this weird and often murderous practice, there are also reports of lecturers engaging in the unwholesome practices as well. What was hitherto introduced in the early days, as extra-curricular engagement to promote academic fraternity amongst like-minded students of creative science has recently, simply been transformed into ritualistic organizations in Nigerian universities without much ado.

The pride displayed by Pan-Africanists emphasizing the glory of African witches and the feats they are claimed to perform by e.g. commanding the demise of a tree before the watchful eyes of admirers almost seems to tell any unsuspecting beholder that Africa has a specific science of its own, which sharply contrasts with academic science as the world knows it. African friends that were privately interviewed by me for the purpose of this exposé will show no restraint in identifying the involvement of witches in the misfortune affecting any other African colleague within their fold even in Europe so far away from home. At the same time, they will explain that the power of witches is reduced if not almost terminated when they are compelled to fly the long distance across the Atlantic in any nocturnal journey. One Nigerian lady once told me this fairy tale without mincing words that there is something about the Atlantic that strips witches of their powers when they fly across it in the night since witches only fly at night.

I remember the case of a good African lady friend of mine in Germany who lived on the fast lane with "Drugs, Sex and Rock'n Roll" as we use to say in jovial moods! In the ultimate end, this lady shockingly dropped dead within the confines of her toilet on one routine day in the aftermath of an overdose. A few days later, reports reached me of some of her friends and relatives who went to the hospital asking German doctors to allow them access to the lady to remove some of her body parts for sacrifices to appease the gods. Of course, I was told they were politely denied the privilege due to concerns over the legal implication of such an act in Germany.

So strong is the belief of the average African in the powers of the gods, spirits and sorcery that the mitigating impact of school education on these beliefs remains simply marginal. In the end, the only science that has steadily progressed in Africa, is the science of performing sacrifices to the gods and the spirits. Western countries have advanced beyond several imaginable limits improving the well-being of mankind and breaking all historical grounds. The hardcore African will still pride himself with mysteries yet uncovered in Africa. He will tell a tale of how our ancestors became this and overcame that! By this means and by that means and again, bla, bla, bla! He will forget that the inventor of the aircraft or the simple short gun that fascinated the Africans at the Cape of Good Hope (courtesy of "King Solomon's Mines") were created by folks at another end of the world, who also did not have many resources at their disposal but the call of necessity.

Today, some Africans in the East of the Blackman's continent will run after Albinos to kill them for sacrifices in the belief that their body parts have magical powers. The parts are then sold to witch doctors, who then make so-called miracle charms and medicines from them. Tom Odula reporting from Nairobi, Kenya for the Huffington Post on November 28, 2009 explains that a complete dismembered set of an albino body can fetch up to $75,000 and Tom being an indigenous Kenyan knows precisely what he was talking about.[57]

The epicenter of this human explosion in the hunt for albinos is Tanzania. Records show that between 2007 and 2009 at least 50 albinos were killed in Tanzania. As at 2009, a headcount uncovered a figure of 10,000 albinos that were displaced after going into hiding to avoid the bounty killers. This was reported by the International Federation of the Red Cross and the Red Crescent. One Jeb Sharp who reported for "The World" from Dar-Es-Salam in Tanzania on June 10, 2010 recounted as follows:

"One person, a little boy of 4 was murdered. A man lost a hand, the hand was chopped off. A little girl who is now in hospital, her hand was chopped off and there was an attack with severe injuries when a woman of 33 years of age and a little girl of 12 months old were attacked."[58)]

Indeed, in spite of the evils and justifiable condemnation of the "Whiteman" for the crimes against humanity that he committed against the Blackman in imperialist and colonial history, it is yet the Whiteman's science that performed researches and explained to the world in the establishment of biological facts, the reason behind the difference in the looks of the Albino. Biology teaches us that a genetic defect responsible for pigment insufficiency is the reason for the albino's skin color and the poor adaptation of the albino's skin to normal environmental conditions. The self-styled East African scientific explanation of the albino's condition however, is influenced by the gods, the witches, the spirits and supernatural powers.

The Acquired Immune Deficiency Syndrome (AIDS) was discovered as an epidemy in the small Ugandan fishing village of Kasensero about 33 years ago. In the absence of scientific research and probes, it was initially, generally believed that the victims were afflicted by the curse of Munteego locally regarded as being lethal enough to wipe off entire families.

Only years later were foreign scientists able to prove to this village and the entire nation that this sickness that everyone knew as "Slim" was a new disease that had nothing to do with any curse or spiritual affliction.[(59)]

Summarizing the general mentality of the African in his belief in supernatural powers, Vicky Ntetema, a former BBC journalist who reported on the killing of Albinos, had this to say:

"These witch doctors have turned into small gods. All over the place people fear them, people believe them. People trust them. If you say to a Tanzanian you don't have to go to witch doctor to be successful you don't have to go to a witch doctor to solve your problems they will look at you and say are you coming from Mars? Most of them believe in witch doctors."[(58)]

That is true of very many Africans across the entire continent.

Amid huge skepticism, Africa embraced Christianity. In fact, a close watch on Christianity in Africa today may uncover the brutal reality that the average African does not believe in Christianity for the sheer love of Jesus Christ of Nazareth – a location in Israel that only sounds musical to his ears. The vast majority of African Christians believe in Christianity as an opposing force to the powers of witches in the realms of Satan. Unlike the European for whom Satan simply represents evil, the African associates evil in a very concrete sense, with the powers of witches and evil spirits, and that is a major driving force in the acceptance of Christianity. In some cases, the heathen life of the animists often requiring expensive items for sacrifices to appease the gods as demanded by hungry and fraudulent witch doctors, simply prove to be too expensive and ill affordable for comfort. In the end, Christianity turns out to be less expensive. Africa today, thus has different brands of Christianity, some modified to suit the unique African pattern. Much more than the inventors of this religion in Europe and the Middle East however, the fraudulent aspect of Christianity is what the African seems to handle best.

* * * * *

Chapter 6

African Churches and the Sanctification of Crimes

In this chapter, we will attempt to identify the peasant folks in Africa as a chessboard pawn played by different groups to advance selfish interests. We will treat our central theme from one other perspective. It has so far, not been difficult to identify the uneducated or poorly educated folks as the central constituency of traditional institutions. A constituency that is systematically nurtured to believe strongly in the supernatural superiority of traditional institutional monarchies to keep the monarchs ever important and relevant to public life! It never seems to matter what price the folks pay in collective retarded political and intellectual growth. In this chapter, we will see the black African folks as a pawn in the hands of celestial and self-ordained cardinals, bishops and prophets of *doom and destruction* representing the kingdom of God on earth!

Nowhere in the world is the saying that *"Religion is the opium of the masses"* more true of Christianity than in Africa. Fanatic Christianity in Africa is only paralleled by fanatic Mohammedanism in the Middle East and parts of Africa and Asia even though devoid of the jihadist element prevalent in Islam. Indeed, fanatical attachment to the Christian religion and the teachings of Jesus Christ is not confined to Africa alone. Christianity for committed Christians all over the world, most prominently in the American continent, is about the belief in the teachings of Jesus Christ as the sole means of human salvation. The truly committed Christian can hardly be swayed by any argument that seeks to divert from blind faith in biblical teachings. The need to take a critical and scientific view in evaluating the religion as Professor Stephen Hawking would do is not an issue for the committed believer. Rightly so too! After all, it is within the democratic and constitutional confines of individual rights to believe whatever he/she chooses. But there is nowhere else in the whole "wild" world where churches and church leaders hardly have any other function but to fill a socio-psychological gap in a world dominated by the pervasive fear of imaginary supernatural powers but Africa. Nowhere else in the world do church leaders have the status of substitutes for witch doctors and spiritual healers than in Africa.

For the purpose of setting the records straight though, there are also true and authentic Christian Believers in the project of Jesus in Africa much like their counterparts in different parts of the world.

Believers who take the teachings of the Bible as fully as they are served! Faithful followers who hold on firmly to the belief that Jesus Christ came to this world, having been born in miraculous circumstances without carnal biological processes! Faithful followers who are unshaken in their common belief that Jesus did not only rise from death proceeding straight up to the realms of God in heaven above the cloud but also died for the sins of man!

These are believers for whom the worldly views of a neutral observer would mean nothing. The atheist who will claim that Jesus did not die to wash away his sins will mean nothing to the ardent believer in the teachings of Jesus.

In societies dominated by the rampaging influence of witch-doctors and a general psyche inspired by awe and fear of spirits and supernatural forces however, the setting is different. The compelling potential of a total and collective submission to a life shaped by an understanding of clairvoyance and spiritual obsession is the centerpiece of life in such societies. That indeed, is what Africa is made of. In such societies, there is also a compelling counter-potential for resistance and rebellion, not the least, when the cost of sacrifices to appease the gods and spirits approach horrendous dimensions. Consequently, the search for an alternative power becomes an automatic process. An alternative of convenience!

In the unfortunate absence of scientific statistics however, indicative social trends and visible characteristics obviously show the teeming majority of African Christians as Believers borne out of strategic necessity. The need to find a more widely acceptable and presentable alternative to superstition, animism and the heathen life of wallowing in the realms of idols, sacrifices and weird beliefs seems to dictate the shape and quality of the belief in Jesus Christ! This can be seen against the backdrop of the dichotomy in the beliefs cladding the practice of idol worshipping and the African Traditional Religions. On the one hand, practitioners of the African traditional religions are generally looked down upon as being largely uneducated and thus holding on more strongly to the heritage of their ancestors than do their educated counterparts. On the other hand though, the educated elite often emphasize the need to uphold Africa's cultural heritage as the cornerstone of Pan-Africanism. Occultists and witch doctors are therefore sometimes openly encouraged not to be ashamed of being who they are. At the same time though, there is also a subtle sense of being on the wrong side of the educational divide in openly claiming occultism, witchcraft or idol worshipping as one's religion. Yet this heathen religion has a very strong following as our preceding analyses have shown. Followers include politicians, the ordinary folk and as we seek to elaborate further down this discourse, very many self-proclaimed pastors, bishops and church leaders practicing the superstitious religion behind closed doors

It is therefore not uncommon, while completing official forms for employment or any other purpose, to find almost no single African writing "Pagan",

"Heathen" or "Occultist" wherever questions on religion are asked. Many would rather write "Christian" or "Moslem".

This automatically brings us to the reality of the inevitable classification of African Christians. For the purpose of this work, I will differentiate between the "True Believers" and "The Instrumental Believers". While the former is very difficult to come by if at all existent, the latter category litters the streets of every African society like sand on the beach. The instrumental believer in Christianity includes those who regard the religion and its leaders as alternative but positive witchcraft and witches and thus embrace the instrumental rationality of taking refuge with the religion. In addition to the innocent and earnest seeker of a calm life in peace and orderliness, the instrumental believer also includes criminals and fraudsters seeking God's protection from exposure to law enforcement. We should also not forget the numerous fraudulent preachers of God's words for pecuniary, selfish and personal gains.

In the introduction to his proposed work that was never published *"A Contribution to the Critique of Hegel's Philosophy of Right"*, Karl Marx wrote in 1843:

"Man makes religion, religion does not make man. Religion is, indeed, the self-consciousness and self-esteem of man who has either not yet won through to himself, or has already lost himself again."[(60)]

In the continued analysis of the tragic contribution of religion to the prevalent level of intellectual and academic growth in Africa, the accuracy of this Karl Marx's observation as if tailor-made for the African societies, will be seen in its entire package as a matter-of-course without having to be a Marxist. Just one commonly expressed view by African Christians will take us one step closer into this quest. It will help us understand the depth of intellectual dysfunction brought to bear on the African society by obsession with religion and the notion of redemption and the Kingdom of God. Leading African Churchmen often claim that:

"Africa today may be more deprived than the rest of the world in terms of affluence and development, but is far more spiritually advanced than the rest of the world."

Spiritual advancement in this sense, meaning convergence with the Kingdom of God! In other words, sufferings and hardships are one huge cross that the African may need to bear in worldly travails to be able to reap the benefits of God's Kingdom at the end of life. On the face of it, this is a typical religious appeal that is basically not out of the ordinary by global standards. Unfortunately however, millions of suffering people in Africa, pin their hopes on this unfortunate belief in societies marred by a clear shortage of practical creativity in scientific and technological thinking.

For one brand of the African instrumental believer, Christianity is the last hope in a world gone berserk. He is surrounded by robberies, kidnappings and other forms of crime. He lives in a world of con artists with self-proclaimed witch doctors prescribing unaffordable sacrifices to appease "rampaging spirits". He is unable to pay the witch doctor's bills after being told of impending calamities from the spirit world that he truly believes in. He is unable to afford the hospital bill when he takes ill with diagnoses that hardly allow for any picnic mood. The witch doctor cannot help. The medical doctor cannot help. The instrumental believer then takes his final refuge in Christianity and believes that he has now found the ultimate solace that is affordable to him financially and psychologically. All he needs to do is to believe that Jesus Christ died for his sins. He is told that this belief alone wipes away all worries, sicknesses and poverties. Diseases are healed through prayers and belief. Poverty is wiped away only if the belief is strong enough. Anything wrong in the process of redemption is proof of weakness in the faith reposed in Jesus Christ.

The church and its leaders now replace the witch doctors. The visions seen by the pastor replaces the messages of the witch doctor that were conveyed from ancestral spirits after consulting oracles and supposedly meeting in the coven of witches. This time however, the pastor conveys his own visions "directly" from God in heaven. The sacrifices that the believer could not afford for the appeasement of spirits and gods are now replaced by the voluntary 'offerings' of his rare cash to the purses of the church and its leaders. If he still takes ill or suffers any other misfortune in spite of all efforts, he will readily attribute this either to weakness in his faith, divine punishment for something he may have done wrong or simply to evil forces capitalizing on the weakness of his faith that he will struggle ever harder to strengthen if he is not consumed by the current misfortune.

This is the picture of a man who is completely lost. It is the picture of a man looking for different ways to "win" *through to himself* as Karl Marx says, having truly lost himself in psychologically laborious transit. Every attempt to enlighten the mind of this true instrumental believer using scientific arguments on the normality of human life processes that neither Jesus nor the witch doctor can change will be tantamount to robbing him of his last hope built on fantasies and illusion. On this, Karl Marx says:

"To call on them (Believers) to give up their illusions about their condition is to call on them to give up a condition that requires illusions. The criticism of religion is, therefore, in embryo, the criticism of that vale of tears of which religion is the halo ... Criticism has plucked the imaginary flowers on the chain not in order that man shall continue to bear that chain without fantasy or consolation, but so that he shall throw off the chain and pluck the living flower."[60]

It therefore hardly comes as any surprise that con artists finally take advantage of the market niche. The church business has been discovered and rediscovered several times in many African societies. Yet the sector is waxing ever stronger. Self-proclaimed Pastors, Over-"Seers" and founders of churches are growing ever richer while many followers do not seem to care that they themselves are growing ever poorer.

Flock of Fraudulent Churches and Church Leaders

The Nigerian SUN newspaper carried a headline on January 20, 2012. The headline reads "Horror in Oshogbo". The report provided a sordid account of an irate mob of youths in the western Nigerian city of Oshogbo razing down a church that had been in existence for over 30 years. Readers were served the story of followers who regarded the founder of their church as their "god and savior". The founder (Jacob Adebayo Oladele) had died more than twenty years to the date of the protest but the church reportedly built a cult around his remains which they continued to worship assiduously. The alleged mysterious spiritual operations of the church centers around *"vital parts of the human body ... allegedly discovered inside the church"* including human skulls.[61] Timely intervention by law enforcement agents reportedly averted the lynching of the church members.

This extreme model of combining traditional religion with the practice of Christianity to facilitate or ease the performance of outlandish acts that may qualify as miracles or God-inspired visions is not an uncommon or isolated model in Africa. The setting is after all, a society in which extraordinary occurrences easily go as supernatural and spirit-inspired. The difference is often drawn between the Evil and the Holy Spirit with the actors converging in result as "Over-Seers or Witch doctors"!

While the church leaders prefer to wear the public clad of Holy Spirit guidance, Witch doctors and sorcerers often aspire to showcase themselves as practicing witchcraft for the good of mankind.

Pastors and self-styled divine ambassadors often arouse the interest of potential followers by impressing upon them, their ability to cast away evil spirits and restore lost souls to God in heaven. One Nigerian Isaac Salau is an example of such self-styled *prophets of God* until his deceptive scheme was laid bare in the early months of 2012. This common example of African fraudsters, who have discovered a new avenue of enrichment by taking advantage of popular emotions and religious appeal featured in a court case in the Nigerian metropolis Lagos.

Posing as a "Prophet" (not just a Pastor) before a small-scale business-lady Ms. Franca Iboi – owner of a car-wash business – Isaac Salau and an accomplice, who reportedly disappeared from the radar of law enforcement, promised to cleanse the lady's business premises of evil spirits. Materials required for the prayer and cleansing process were estimated at Naira 600,000 (roughly three thousand Euros) which the lady readily paid upon sighting a spontaneous fire outbreak in a corner of her business premises during a prayer session. When she was however told to sell her car to finance the continued cleansing process however, the lady alerted the police.[62]

While this common example can be dismissed as a mere criminal act that is possible and prevalent in every walk of business life, it can be argued that the method adopted by the conman "Prophet" is downright criminal, primitive and unsophisticated. There is however a number of unknown and unreported cases of smarter preachers and prophets adopting more sophisticated methods that are not easily discovered and the figure can be estimated in horrendous dimensions.

Another daring, audacious and simply preposterous example of all criminal acts in the name of God, will once again, be taken from Nigeria. This time, the setting is in the central Nigerian city of Lokoja. As reported by the Vanguard newspaper of June 20, 2012, the city played host to a popular African Church event called "Deliverance"[63].

Deliverance from sin, from the fangs of evil spirits and the grip of Lucifer is often staged with high-profile fanfare in many African communities. Preachers and miracle healers often rise to prominence in such events. Churches organizing such events often lavish money advertising them on Radio, Television, Newspapers and posters and handouts. Believers stream in en masse to take a touch of holy deliverance often from a preacher-man that only stops short of claiming to be the reincarnation of Jesus Christ.

They will preach forcefully and passionately with 'faith in and commitment to Jesus' seemingly flowing through them from their hair to their toes. They will energize their crowd ratcheting up emotions and ecstasy till the crowd is carried away and bubbling in some holy excitement. They allegedly 'heal' the sick and perform unspeakable 'miracles'. They are 'spiritual' heroes and 'Ambassadors' of the might of Jesus!

At the center of this particular fraud event was a well-established church with several branches in different cities in Nigeria – The Eagle Kingdom Church. One self-styled Bishop Bamidele who heads the Lokoja branch of the Eagle Kingdom Church reportedly appealed to his counterpart in the Port-Harcourt branch of the same church, to help him raise money for the launch of a book he had written. The man he approached – Pastor Chuks – was reported to be an expert conman in such fraudulent creativities.[63]

Pastor Chuks simply got his skilled team together to practice a routine act that they were probably not doing for the first time. His team comprising a lady that was unfortunately allegedly born as a Mermaid also featured people who were supposedly deaf and dumb. Some were allegedly afflicted with unspeakable illnesses. The trick was simple. These talented actors were to be healed during the 'Deliverance' show to put the divine powers of Pastor Chuks on show.[63]

This indeed, is not an isolated example. In a society that offers fertile grounds for the growth of fantastic illusions, there is hardly any readiness to question the authenticity of things that should ordinarily have gone down as unrealistic and stupefying. On the contrary, rather than accepting fraudulent healings and miracles for what they are, the average African Christian will quote sections of the Bible to justify the authenticity of fraud claiming that the Bible foresaw the emergence of con artists to discredit the consistency of authentic miracles. They are readily termed the fulfillment of the prophecy. They never mind that the Jewish society from which Jesus originates handles such fantastic tales of dubious tidings with extreme caution. Believers in the Jewish religion hardly accept claims of miracles, which the ordinary Israeli will readily qualify as mere magic. They will tell anyone that the nation of Israel was awash with the likes of Jesus Christ in his days, performing so-called miracles. The average African Christian will report that the Bible had already told the world that a prophet is never accepted in his own home. But they forget that Prophet Mohammed first enjoyed and still enjoys maximum acceptance in his homeland Saudi Arabia, before his credibility was sold to the rest of the world. The average African Christian will do everything to wipe away obvious contradictions in the holy book to buttress his beliefs and sustain his world of illusions – "...the vale of tears of which religion is the halo"[60].

Luck however ran out on Pastor Chuks on the fateful day of "Deliverance" as one sober observer and believer refused to be swayed by the fantastic replication of the miracles of Jesus Christ. This observer alerted the police who swung into action and rounded up the fraudsters. The police arrested 7 fake pastors and paraded them before the media in the typical Nigerian prelude to justice.[63]

During the question and answer session in the media parade, Pastor Chuks called off the bluff and was quoted as saying: *"This is not robbery, it's pure professionalism. Every profession has its own way of surviving. The police have their own way, the lawyers have their own way; even you journalists have your own way; what I did is pure business and survival instinct."*
[63]

Pastor Osita Chukwu (female) who played the role of a Mermaid reported having been promised Naira 16,000 (about € 80.00) with a down-payment of N 1,000 pending the conclusion of the "Deliverance" show.

There are a lot more other fraudulent "Revival" and "Deliverance" programs staged very frequently in several African societies that are more intelligently packaged and executed with more sophistication that the fraud is never exposed. Reference can as well be made to *"Shocking Findings of a Research on Ghanaian Pastors"* written by Emmanuel Sarpong Owusu-Ansah.[64] Poor peasants donate their scarce and hard-earned money in excitement and conviction after such events following breathtaking but fake and misleading miracles and outstanding achievements. The benefactors at the end of the day are always the pastors and self-proclaimed emissaries of God taking full advantage of the general ignorance in the comfort of their overwhelming material abundance.

It does not stop at that. Playing the exorcist card, these self-proclaimed agents of God do everything they can to impress their superior spiritual status upon their unsuspecting followers. They will often mumble a bunch of incomprehensible and non-decipherable nonsensical utterances on their pulpit claiming to be talking in tongues with God speaking a language directly through them that only the spirits can understand. Their continued survival in the profession depends after all, in the acceptance of their spiritual superiority by the congregation and unsuspecting followers.

This is in very sharp contrast to Christian followership in any randomly chosen European community. So unassuming and ordinary do preachers appear in their pulpit in any European society that they are differentiated from their listeners only by what they wear during church services. Else, on ordinary days, they are as simple, poor or rich as the case may be, and as ordinary as every other member of the religious community. The flamboyant African preacher on the other hand, dresses in designer suits, drives luxurious cars and in very many cases, own private jets with some even boasting aloud that *"My God is not a poor God"* and therefore do not see any reason why they should be poor. They often forget that their followers on whose back such stupendous wealth is built, are poor followers.

In a phenomenon similar to that of the Stockholm syndrome, these poor followers who are supposedly the victims and captives of this willful and wanton exploitation turn out to be the defenders of the blossoming preachers. It is not unusual to hear such church goers and congregation members ridiculing pastors who appear outwardly poor. Such followers would pride themselves with the projected richness of their own pastors boasting of the success of the congregation in taking good care of its pastor. They will deride poor pastors for not offering sufficient inspiration to potential followers to join the congregation, using the external show of wealth as a source of inspiration to join the congregation.

"My sister, have you seen the pastor of that church around the corner? Have you seen how wretched he looks? Seeing his poverty, you will even be discouraged to join his church" they will often say.

It may be recalled that the phenomenon of the Stockholm syndrome or Capture-bonding came to light in August 1973. The bank *Kreditbanken* in the Normalmstrong district of Stockholm in Sweden was robbed on August 23, 1973 with several bank employees held hostage in the bank vault until they were freed on August 28, 1973. The paradox of the drama was such that *"the victims became emotionally attached to their captors, rejected assistance from government officials at one point and even defended them (hostage takers) after they were freed from their six-day ordeal."* [65]

The term was referred to for the first time, by the Criminologist and Psychiatrist Nils Bejerot who assisted the Police in the investigations. It is further explained that this gave birth to *"a psychological phenomenon in which hostages express empathy and have positive feelings towards their captors, sometimes to the point of defending them. These feelings are generally considered irrational in light of the danger or risk endured by the victims, who essentially mistake a lack of abuse from their captors for an act of kindness".*[65]

In the bigger picture however, the African followers of the Christian faith with a huge focus on visions, spirits and direct communication with God, fall prey to a different model of psychological hostage taking and incarceration within the limits of a free world. Church leaders and pastors who feed on the trickle-down handouts from the middle class and poor members of the congregation, are celebrated as powerful heroes of the community on the understanding that they are kind and helpful to the community of followers with their God-given power over evil spirits. It does not matter at all that no one truly knows what an evil spirit or a holy spirit is. At the same time though, there will be no shortage of African Christians who will come out at any given time to narrate their encounter with spirits of different kinds.

The multifold resurgence or rebirth of Jesus Christ has indeed, being recorded in different parts of Africa at different points in time. In addition to media reports to this effect, I have personally witnessed a fellow in my old neighborhood in Africa claiming to be Jesus reborn until he was taken into custody for psychiatric attention. The last known high-profile case of the 35-year old South African Hindu woman from Durban Katherine Jhawarelall, who claimed to have been the reincarnation of Jesus came to the limelight in 2006. This lady, who holds a Bachelor degree in Sociology and Criminology from the University of South Africa, claims to have sensations or pains alongside bodily marks in spots corresponding to the crucifixion wounds of Jesus. But Jesus was not the only person crucified on the cross in the ancient Jewish tradition. Execution by crucifixion was the norm in those days in the Jewish society. If the story of reincarnation was true in any sense, why was it not someone else but Jesus that she was re-enacting in reincarnation? She backs her claims with a series of unverifiable spiritual and physical variables. Yet questions abound endlessly.[66]

In fact, since the issue of Jesus is taken extremely seriously by the African Christian, any preacher-man who comes out to declare himself a reincarnation of Jesus Christ is usually perceived as taking the game one step too far.

This deterrent impact seems to have stopped several testimonies in the African world from revealing the rebirth of Jesus Christ in different African societies in the present day. Else, in its current world of sophisticated conmen, Africa would have been left to face the choice of determining which Jesus is for real in a tale of religious ridicule. It should be added in all fairness though, that the second, third and endless coming of Jesus has been replicated multifold also in other parts of the world. The online Encyclopedia Wikipedia lists not less than 30 examples.

Just one footnote on the lighter side: one of the interesting highlights and probably the peak of sensationalism marking the human element in the propagation of the Christian religion was recorded in November 2010, when one South African Pastor Xola Skosana of Cape Town's Khayelitsha township declared that Jesus Christ was HIV positive.[67]

Exorcising evil spirits

Sometime in December 2011 an event was brought to public attention in Nigeria that was reportedly recorded in 2009. It was a scene in a Nigerian church that brought rights activists and concerned citizens up in arms. At the center of the controversy was a very popular Church known for its nationwide spread and international appeal – the *Winners Chapel* also known as the *Living Faith Church*. Its ultimate leader is a celebrity amongst his African followers and often referred to by them, as "Papa". The Winner Chapel was described by the British online news site Mail Online as *"part of a worldwide empire of evangelical ministries run by Nigeria's wealthiest preacher David Oyedepo who has an estimated £93 million fortune, a fleet of private jets and a Rolls-Royce Phantom."* Branches of the church are reported as growing rapidly over several cities in the United Kingdom in a massive recruitment drive.[68]

Pastor David Oyedepo in a characteristic African pattern bears the self-imposed title of a Bishop. Bishops, Overseers, Prophets and Redeemers are common titles arbitrarily used by African Preachers. The only title that African Christian leaders have so far not awarded to themselves arbitrarily, is simply that of the "Pope". Oyedepo is often dubbed the 'Pastorpreneur' by experts of the scene depicting him as a form of 'entrepreneurial preacher' on the road for "Jesus" but never for his pocket. Pastor Oyedepo runs an empire of business interests among which is the airline called Dominion Air.[69]

On one fateful day in 2009, Pastor Oyedepo was on a routine mission in the church's headquarters in Otta – a city in western Nigeria. Several young ladies had lined up the pulpit on their knees waiting for deliverance prayer. For the pastor, they were just witches that had just one duty to perform in front of him, namely confess to their witchcraft and nefarious nocturnal activities. He was the star of the day! The deliverer that everyone looked up to! He had called upon the sinners to come forward for "Deliverance" in the mighty name of Jesus!

Unfortunately for him though, one courageous teenage girl of Eastern Nigerian origin resisted the stigmatization before the gaze of hundreds of other worshippers, media men and camera crews that were characteristic features of appearances made by this celebrity preacher man with self-proclaimed healing abilities.[70] The young girl declared *"I am not a witch. My own witch is for Jesus"*. The visibly stunned Pastor Oyedepo asked *"You're what?"* Upon hearing a repeat of what the girl said, he responded *"You're a foul devil"* adding that Jesus Christ has no witches and gave this young teenage girl a slap on her left temple. This was caught on camera and the footage went viral on YouTube. At the time he met the next girl on the row who refused to play out the script of his stardom by also saying she is not a witch, the pastor could not go on distributing slaps. He declared all the liars before the pulpit cut down without much ado! In the aftermath, political activism followed. Child molestation was alleged. Signatures were gathered for prosecution, etc. As is the case with the rich and powerful in several African societies however, not much was made of the case. Not even an instance of prosecution investigations in the interest of the public was noted for the records. There was no single government reaction through the Attorney-General and Minister of Justice.

For the sake of comparison, late Michael Jackson dangled his little baby within the firm grips of his hands through the windows of a hotel in Berlin for some split seconds, to show the media his latest pride in reproduction. It was on November 20, 2002. The aftermath was a gruesome nightmare for the King of Pop. Rights activists all over the world were up in arms and the institution of public prosecution had to launch investigations in Germany to determine if the law had been broken. Yet Michael Jackson meted no abuse or bodily harm on his child. The King of

Pop had to make sincere public apologies and release a clear explanation of his intention and love for his child to quell a long-standing media furor that surely took its toll on his wellbeing and state of mind. In Nigeria however, a clear physical attack on a child goes unpunished when the perpetrator is rich and powerful.[71]

An activist Attorney Robert Igbinedion took up the case of Pastor (self-styled Bishop) Oyedepo and filed for damages in a local court seeking to get Naira 2 billion (about €10 million) awarded to the victim as damages.[72] For some unexplainable reasons, the young courageous lady who was filmed at the height of the pastor's show of shame, became a ghost figure who could not be found to testify before the court. It still remains a mystery if intimidation played any role. In the end though, the case was dismissed in July 2012 and as usual, the rich and powerful culprit walked away scot-free while the private attorney was compelled to pay the public offender (often styled the richest Nigerian Pastor) N 20,000 (about €100.00) as awarded by the court. Nothing was heard about public prosecution while the judgment in question is being appealed at the time of going to press.

Referring to the slapping incident that made news also in England, a Labor MP Paul Flynn remarked thus:

"What is also alarming is the reported violence and the lack of respect for the status of women. It's taking us back to a previous age of ignorance and prejudice that we all thought the church had escaped."[73]

This is very much in sharp contrast to the deafening silence of politicians within Nigeria, where the offence itself was committed. There are after all, several politicians prostrating before this man of God for his miraculous blessings and spiritual assistance. It did not matter any bit to Nigerian politicians that media investigations uncovered facts to underscore charges of the financial exploitation of members of the Winner Chapel congregation. Members are reportedly handed payment slips upon entering the London branch of the church asking them to make cash payment donations or use checks or debit cards. Donations to the Winners Chapel in England between 2006 and 2010 almost doubled from £2.21 million to £4.37 million.[73]

The sense of exuberance with which African Christian preachers prosecute their campaign of cleansing society of witchcraft within the realms of the egocentric promotion of stardom as exorcists brings us back to the issue we addressed at the start of this discourse. Another self-styled Nigerian Bishop Sunday Williams had declared sometime in 2008 that the Nigerian State of Akwa-Ibom was a coven for witches and had *"roughly 2.3 million witches and wizards ... and most of them are children"*. [33] Till the present day, the method of collating such daring statistics remains a mystery that is strongly guarded by this self-styled Bishop of non-scientific statistics.

The claim alone made by this preacher man that he had killed 110 of such witches was not enough to spur public prosecution investigators into action.[33]

African Communities Overseas

As Pastor Oyedepo's example indicates, the case of exploitative, stupefying and fanatical religious commitment and practices is very much the same for black Africans living in different societies outside the shores of Africa. Ordinarily, the psychological impact of exposure to foreign societies with their inherent cultural and traditional differences boosts expectations that beneficial informal education may play a role in shaping the perception and world view of the lucky few at the center of such exposures. As already hinted above severally, dwindling economic fortunes in Africa alongside the desperation for survival has driven millions of black Africans to seek a new beginning in more affluent and advanced societies. While a sizeable number of the female population of such sojourners from specific areas of Africa such as Nigeria (most prominently) and Ghana engages in prostitution, a sizeable number of the male population (mostly from Nigeria) engages in drug businesses and fraudulent activities. It should be highlighted at this juncture and for the avoidance of doubt that Nigeria, which clearly tops the list of criminal activities committed by Africans in several foreign societies, does have a huge number of progressive, intelligent and very productive citizens also living in foreign societies. Intellectual male and female Nigerians running several white-collar management projects in academia as well as those actively practicing reputable professions in many foreign countries are no rarities. Unfortunately however, since empty vessels always make the loudest noise, the noises of the prostitutes, human traffickers, drug smugglers and scam artists ring the loudest in the corridors of law enforcement.

Be that as it may though, with some goodwill, a lot is easily attributed to the escape from poverty and the overwhelming responsibility of coping with new challenges. It is expected that time will play the trick of blending minds with the reality of new societies and new challenges beginning from adaptation to languages.

Unfortunately however, a large section of African communities craves the notion of self-encapsulation. It is not uncommon in several European, Asian and American cities to find black African communities living almost in voluntary isolation from their host societies. They deny themselves the opportunity of uplifting the generally poor educational background brought from home through a smart and strategic blending with new cultural and social values. They will claim to be protecting unique identities, which ordinarily is a laudable venture. Since the venture to uphold unique identities is not practiced and executed within the proper mix that may be beneficial to overall progress however, the result is an even more confused and unfocused mindset.

Africans thus end up establishing secret societies amongst themselves within their host communities. They will nurture their own self-styled witch doctors and regularly call home for active family commitment to spiritual protection and the importation of amulets, Talisman, charms and magical objects to their host societies often leaving custom inspectors puzzled at the definition of objects before their eyes. Practices of this sort are indeed the prelude to the example already given above of a group of Africans going to a German hospital requesting permission from hospital authorities to remove some body parts of their deceased colleague for ritualistic purposes.

The Africans will worship in makeshift churches created by them and which are characteristically different from what they see in their host societies. They will raise pastors from within their fold to see visions and perform miracles for them the way they know from home. I remember one African church in London with a "visionist" African Preacher. Members of his congregation held him in high esteem for what they considered the accuracy of the visions that he saw. One particular vision caught my attention after an unsuspecting young woman came out of victimization unscathed. She was a pretty looking Sierra Leonean acquaintance of mine. She explained to me in a private conversation how this London pastor approached her suddenly after one Sunday service. He had intimated her of a vision that he had seen very recently fresh from God's own megaphone. He had seen biological misfortunes coming the way of my friend in her quest to conceive a child. She was to have difficulties in reproduction, so the vision uncovered. God had allegedly revealed to the pastor that my friend, who was already a mother of two and longed to have one more child, will have difficulties getting pregnant again. If she eventually did, she was likely to die in the process of giving birth. The only solution recommended by the pastor was fasting and prayers but not in the confines of her own home. He recommended to my friend to camp out in the church for seven days fasting and praying intensively with the help of the pastor. She had barely camped in the church for three days when she realized that the motives of the pastor who sought to have carnal knowledge of her was to invoke God's blessing for unison between them both. After all, what God has put together, no man can put asunder. I could laugh over it when I heard the story but for my friend, the story was not amusing at all.

Africans will habitually ensure that their pastor lives big on their offerings submitted on Sundays during church services. It will not matter to them that the practice of Christianity before their very eyes in the host society they are living in focuses basically, on upholding moral values and spiritual benevolence. They will subject themselves to exploitation from the pastors that they have nurtured with their own sweat and claim to have a better understanding of Christianity than their host society does. It will not matter to them for instance that King James who authorized the version of the Bible that they hang on to was a former King of Great Britain. The black African will claim spiritual superiority even over

King James and the Pope. They will clap and dance themselves into ecstasy during church services lasting the whole day on a Sunday until the neighborhood feels disturbed and requests police intervention. It will not matter to them that Sunday services that they see in their host communities never last beyond two or three hours to allow citizens time to attend to other businesses of the day. In a nutshell, the average African community overseas shuts itself off from its host community to re-live a mini-Africa in a community from whose infrastructural, economic and intellectual organization it seeks to profit.

In the end, incessant conflict with neighbors fuels deeper racial detestations in a society that is naturally and inherently cautious in its contacts with the African that it knows with negative prejudices through media coverage. The African thus ends up being driven deeper down his own encapsulation often with cries of racial victimization exacerbated by his own actions. Weird practices by the self-styled witch doctors and self-styled priests and pastors often end up in conflicts with the law which in turn, spark some rude awakening.

Regrettably however, whenever they return to their native African home for visits or other purposes, these type of Africans living in encapsulated Diaspora are often loudest in attempting to showcase their financially, culturally and often, non-existent educationally uplifted status to the local folks. Those from England or America will attempt to elevate themselves above the environment of their upbringing by feigning the British and American accent while speaking English often posing as being so much at home with the English language that they have lost fluency in their own native language. They never mind though that they live in encapsulation abroad and speak their native language and the Pidgin English with their own folks in the Diaspora almost 24/7.

Sometime in November 2011, the world woke up to a rude shock when the media reported in Britain, how a self-ordained Nigerian miracle healer leading a charlatan shamanic church in Britain (and there are many of such) sent at least six HIV-infected patients to their early graves.

Nigerian celestial and evangelical churches in London, Manchester, Birmingham and even Glasgow in Scotland had publicized their ability to cure HIV and AIDS with the mighty power of Jesus. Once every month, the churches held mass prayer sessions for deliverance and miracles. These are events in which "Witches" come forward to confess. Patients who are "healed" by the miracle of prayers and the power of Jesus also come out to testify.

In this specific case though, the British television news channel "Sky News" sent three undercover reporters to the "Synagogue Church of all Nations" (SCOAN) in Southwark, South London led by one Pastor T. B. Joshua. Patients of HIV responded to calls to come forward for divine healing. The reporters recorded assurances that all patients can be healed. All they needed to do was to provide documentary proof that they truly suffered HIV infection. They were reportedly filmed before and after their testimonies with the footage posted on the churches website (www.scoan.org) to buttress the Churches superior healing power.

Healing was reportedly done with the pastor shouting over the person being healed commanding the devil to come out of the body in the typical fashion of exorcism. Water is then sprayed in the patient's face. One of the undercover reporters named Shatila, was indeed also HIV positive.

"I was told if I had faith, everything would be fine, and because of my faith, I would be cured of HIV. ... All I needed was to believe that the HIV in my body would go away." Shatila wrote.[74]

Reporting further online on November 27, 2011, the *International Business Times* stated:

"The pastors told Shatila that she would know she had been cured because after you have been prayed for and anointed with holy water during the special Sunday service, you will experience some pains in your body or pass urine more frequently or have some diarrhea. This, they said, means the HIV is coming out of your body."[74]

But diarrhea, pains and frequent passing of urine are known symptoms of HIV. Patients were then advised to discontinue usage of administered medications because they had been healed. In fact, the International Business Times quoted Sky News as saying: *"Many churches, including SCOAN, also tell people that they can feel free to have unprotected sex and start a family — and some have infected their partners with HIV as a result."*[(74)]

Sky News finally discovered that at least 6 patients died after they had discontinued using their medications. The British Department of Health reacted and cautioned that *"Faith and Prayer are not a substitute for any form of treatment especially for HIV treatment."*[(74)]

Though the pastors of this church later defiantly released a statement denying any such process in their church claiming they never discouraged the use of medication, the testimony of undercover patients however provided a graphic picture of the despicable self-proclaimed healing powers that the Church never had.

Battle between Witchcraft and Churches of Faith

Today, the battle between the heathen and animist priests, witch doctors and miracle healers on the one hand and the "visionist" Christian preachers talking in tongues and healing poverty and sicknesses in dubious miracles on the other hand, is raging in full force with the commercial pendulum swinging in favor of the Christian fraudsters who are reaping the benefit of *pastorpreneurial* flamboyance. While the witch doctors and self-asserted guardians of the African ancestral powers are unable to make material gains for several reasons, the fortunes of Christian preachers and fraudsters have skyrocketed. Preachers are able to appear sophisticated and educated in their dressings and use of English language and therefore more persuasive as opposed to the often wretched-looking witch doctors in primitive outfits and settings.

ZIMBABWEAN WITCH DOCTOR ©
PHOTO BY HANS HILLEWAERT

The sight of their shrines as our cover picture indicates is an awry sight depicting filth, stench, horror and primitive instincts. It must also be added that the intrinsic and systemic negative disposition of the witch doctors in the scheme of affairs lays a fertile ground for the economic success and popular acceptance that the fraudulent preacher men enjoy. Else, there is no doubting the extensive underground spread and acceptance of the powers of ancestral spirits and witchcraft across all strata of African societies.

Indeed, the most interesting and exciting phase in the lives of the fraudulent preacher men is always the period of ascendance to the chosen profession of divine scamming. It is not uncommon to have active drug users (often marijuana smokers) emerging as pastors. They will use their marijuana-smoking "past" as evidence of their rebirth and exposure to Jesus. Some will even make bold to testify to a life of banditry, murder and other sorts of crime as the prelude to their encounter with Jesus. They are never arrested to account for the crimes they testify to. It will in fact, come as no surprise if many of the self-ordained pastors with wild and weird testimonies simply narrate from hallucinative experiences in some marijuana-induced mental trip. In any case, stories are often told, of encounter with heavenly lights under the shower, the appearance of Jesus in dreams or at riversides including wild and imaginary commands supposedly issued by Jesus to them while floating in some questionable states of mind in the realms of Jah most high.

Watching all these attendant elements of *"...the self-consciousness and self-esteem of (a) man who has either not yet won through to himself, or has already lost himself again"*[(60)] from the neutral vintage point of observation in the Diaspora provides a different thrill of its own altogether.

In the course of my investigations through private interaction with several African hookers in Europe, I have been privy to the weird but customary *modus operandi* of the African mind in the quest to achieve wealth. As already indicated above in the course of this narrative, young African hookers adopt unorthodox solutions in frustrating times of poor patronage by Johns or Punters. They will fall back on parents or other close relatives in Africa to help them out with magical aids from witch doctors to push more Johns and Punters to their sides. In some cases, the names of more successful next-door competitors are simply sent to relations in Africa for onward transmission to witch doctors for supernatural spells to disrupt the fortunes of the successful competitor and turn these fortunes their own way. In fact, I remember one specific instance, in which a young lady sent the name of a rival hooker to her mum for this enhancing magical ritual only for the mother to end up identifying this rival hooker as a close relative hitherto unknown to the lady sending the name for the magical spell.

In the end however visits to the shrines and occultic high-priests by relations in Africa end up producing talismanic objects that are sent to the person demanding them either by mail or through any other known person who may have traveled home on a visit. They always come with instructions for usage to attract the favor of the spirit world to the advantage of the person demanding them. If the talisman comes in the form of soap for showering, specific incantations and prayers are instructed for recitation during usage. If it comes in the form of body cream, the same procedure applies while using the cream. In the form of drinkables and edibles, there are recitations before and after consumption. In other cases, objects are also sent with usage instructions, to deactivate competitors from effective competition. In every instance, payments ranging from €100.00 to €500.0 are required for the services of the medium producing the talisman and charm.

On the other hand, church leaders offer prayers for money and give some do-it-yourself instructions to achieve the desired success.

There was this African hooker who I choose to call "Lady Saw" for the purpose of this narrative. I got acquainted with her and interviewed her informally in a European country in the early 2000s. Like many other hookers in her situation, she had no residence permit to live legally in the European country of her abode. She had escaped her sponsor and pimp and gone underground to start her life from the scratch again having gone weary of selling her body to pay her pimp in an endless process spanning several years. Life underground did not prove beneficial either since she had to escape the cops in any form of control. After trying hard for two years, she was yet unable to find a look alike compatriot to hire residential documents from to present for identification whenever she runs into a police check. She was continuing the process at the time I met her.

Parallel to this however, Lady Saw explored the chances of finding a European man to marry and secure her residential status. This too was proving difficult. Living underground to escape immigration authorities, she claimed a different nationality to make it difficult for the authorities to track her real identity. She got herself registered as a political refugee fleeing political persecution from the country she claimed was hers. These days claiming to be suffering political persecution as a citizen of Nigeria does not sell any more with the European authorities who promptly reject applications for political asylum on this basis. Lady Saw thus did the only thing she could do. She claimed the citizenship of a political hotspot in Africa where political persecution will be easy to believe.

There was also this man she'd been dating for the past two years. Lady Saw could and did not reveal her real identity or her nationality to this man even after two years into their relationship. All the man knew about her was her chosen nickname and the fact that she was a refugee and the citizen of a country she was simply claiming to belong to. The age she declared was also false. He did not know she was a hooker and she had no plans to let him know. On her intention to marry this man however, she was open and honest. The ultimate goal being the acquisition of a legal residential status!

The man was smart and asked a lot of questions. He had no proof of her real name or her nationality and had never seen any identity document to show who she is or who she may be. She had deliberately kept all documents away from him that may cause him to ask further questions. The man would therefore, not marry her under such circumstances. He passed the message over in a brisk and unceremonious phone call.

"Darling, we can remain good friends" he finally told her after futile attempts to be diplomatic and added *"we do not have to marry and we cannot marry. In fact we will have to separate because I have met another woman from the Dominican Republic"* He could hardly finish saying "Republic" when he was sharply interrupted.

"Whhhaaattt?" Lady Saw groaned in awe and consternation with her mobile phone almost falling off her hand. She had told the guy that she would be away to visit her brother in another city and had thus been away since seven days. The truth however, is that she traveled to a different city to work in a brothel and earn a little money. She made up her mind to cut the duration of her stay in the brothel short from the planned 14 days after hearing this horrible news.

"Now wait for me at home. I am coming straight away. I will get home this evening. You just don't know what you're talking about" Lady Saw said in desperation and packed her belongings for the trip back home.

In her desperation however, there was just one last solution that she knows so well: Appeal to divine powers!

Sitting in the train on the home-bound journey, she called her mother in Africa to help out very quickly in these desperate times of ultimate survival. She requested assistance with some remote-controlled spiritual back-up to her horizontal and vertical power of persuasion when she finally gets home.

Get home she did. She wasted no time talking and got down to real business. Amid romantic scenes of red wine, red roses lining the dinner table with delicious meals and tantalizing smell of the latest perfume in town, Lady Saw got her man an unforgettable thrill that ended up with her best in horizontal tricks and acrobatics. Her man missed her badly within the seven days of her absence and made no secret of it. The emotional reunion was one of a kind like the two had never before experienced. The ecstatic moments lasted for three endless days. After three days, it was time for Lady Saw to strike the hammer while the iron was hot.

Her man had however tossed the mental coin over and over again before Lady Saw came back home from her seven-day trip. He had made up his mind. He would not fall victim to the same old trick again.

He vowed to stick to the dictates of his voice of reason. No emotional weakness was to gain the upper hand this time around.

"Darling, we can truly remain good friends" he told Lady Saw again to her second shock within four days. *"The story about the Dominican lady is true. I met her in a virtual chatroom and I visited her in her house while you were away"*

"Are you kidding? Do you know what you're saying? What did you get from her that I am not able to give you?"

"She lives in her own flat darling not in a refugee settlement. I saw her passport, am sure of her name, her age and nationality" the guy said and continued *"Darling, it's not an easy choice to make. I know I cannot do without you. That is why we should remain friends"*

"And how do you expect such a friendship to work out? I need you as my husband not just a friend..."

"I will always be there for you whenever you need me darling. But we cannot be husband and wife"

A clearly devastated Lady Saw was stiffened and dumbfounded and clearly out of her usual self. Neither shouting nor yelling nor throwing of objects around the house or at her man in her characteristic fashion when tempers flare, could help her now. She sat down to focus on the next step to take.

The next day, she called her paternal aunt in Africa and asked for further spiritual assistance since her white guy was proving stubborn. She sought to have combined spiritual forces in addition to the efforts being made by her mum, who had obviously gone consulting one witch doctor after the other. Her paternal aunt suggested the services of a Pastor who should lead her in prayers and miracles.

The next day, her mum called her and asked her to send a minimum of €300.00 for sacrifices prescribed by witch doctors to appease the gods and the spirits to prevail on her estranged boyfriend to make him change his mind very quickly. She ran to the nearest office for telegraphic money transfer and her earnings for one week were reduced by €300.00 plus commission.

When her aunt called her the next day, she was given the telephone number of a pastor that she should call to lead her in prayers and instructions on what to do to have God touch the heart of her boyfriend for a change of heart.

She swung into action immediately and called Pastor James. After the opening niceties and explanation of the problems she was facing in Europe in her quest for a legal residence permit, Pastor James asked Lady Saw pointblank, to pledge a sum of money that she would donate to the church before the services of praying and *visioneering* is embarked upon. Lady Saw pledged €100.00. Thereafter she was told to expect the pastor's call within a few days. The pastor was to fall back on his usual prayerful project to get feedbacks from the Holy Ghost "in the mighty name of Jesus".

Pastor James called back three days later. Lady Saw was advised to enter into a period of fasting to last for seven days. She was to pray three times daily for each of the seven days. In every occasion, she was to strip herself naked within the privacy of her room when her man had gone to work so she could face up to God in the natural mode of her creation. She was to tell God specifically that she has come to him in her natural state asking for the forgiveness of her sins before requesting the favor that God was to do for her. She was not told to face up to the East or the West as she would probably not know which direction would be East or West.

After seven days, she got her man to discuss the same old issue again hoping that the seven-day fasting and naked prayers would have made an impact. She was subjected to another rude awakening when her guy then gave her just seven days to move out of his flat to cement the collapse of their relationship. There and then, she packed her few belongings and her estranged European boyfriend took her in his car to the refugee camp where she shares an assigned room with another African lady, who also works occasionally as a hooker.

It became obvious that neither her mother's travails with witch doctors and voodoo priests could sway her man into blind and overwhelming love for Lady Saw. Matters were made even worse when her aunt called her one week later. Pastor James had complained to the aunt that he was yet to receive €100.00 pledged by Lady Saw. Lady Saw protested helplessly claiming that the prayer did not work. She could therefore not see any reason to pay the pledged €100.00. She was promptly rebuked by her aunt.

"No, no! It's not done that way" the aunt said in a briskly boiling voice *"A pledge is a pledge. It does not matter if the prayer worked or not"*

Weary of starting a personal feud on top of her present frustrations in Europe, Lady Saw agreed to send Pastor James €100.00.

This is a true story that I have narrated with a touch of fiction using only imaginary names and imageries for narrative fluency. It is not an isolated example. Within the typical framework of the Stockholm syndrome, Lady Saw explained away the failure of the prayer and voodoo projects combined. She convinced herself that her faith was not strong enough and that the Atlantic Ocean was an impediment to the efficacy of the powers of witchcraft. She assured me that she would resort to the same solution again whenever the need arises. There are a good number of Africans at home and abroad that will report similar experiences of money for prayer demanded by African pastors.

This throws more light on the field occupied by the ordinary person in a typical black African society. Societies with the Political elite at the top followed by the Economic powerhouses also serving occasionally as powers behind the scene! For some reasons however, these two classes largely submit themselves to the powers of spiritual leaders which they see in witch doctors and church leaders regarding them as the source of their power and continued hold thereupon. We have already commented on African politicians seeking power enhancement from gods and the spirits before animist and voodoo shrines in the belief that they would gain more power from them or uphold the powers that they already have.

Since association with the white-collar image of "Christianity" is more acceptable in polite societies, African political leaders often showcase their association with Pastors and churches. They would often ask citizens to pray for the nation when they fall short of ideas to explain government paralysis and inaction on crucial issues. There was even a reported and flatly denied case of an African leader requesting an Italian company *Gitto Contruzioni General* to renovate a church in his home constituency as a goodwill donation to guarantee the award of a contract.[75]

With the concept of spirits and gods exemplarily accepted through patronage from the top to the bottom of society and hardly any leadership role played by any quarters in critiquing the commercial abuse of the entire concept and system, the ordinary man remains at the receiving end of all forms of exploitation. The business of leading prayers, delivering people from iniquities, delivering messages from God through visions and healing the sick by performing dubious miracles of all sorts are the glaring abuses committed all too commonly and unchallenged. Every attempt to confront such fraud is often always met by claims that the challenger does not know God. A claim that often resonates convincingly when proclaimed publicly amongst Africans since there is never a shortage of Africans who will boldly conclude and declare that NOTHING IS IMPOSSIBLE WITH GOD thus giving a blank check to any self-imposed spiritual fraudster to lay claim to all forms of deceptive and weird miracles! The thin fine line between a healthy religious belief and the realistic bounds of human capabilities is often drowned in the claim that some unknown power beyond human perception is capable of performing every imaginary miracle.

On the other hand, witch doctors and self-proclaimed shamans parade the streets as the factors to be feared over life and death. Church leaders as well as witch doctors exploit the emotional fears and weaknesses of the ordinary man for economic gains. The result – as already highlighted above – is a paradigm shift in favor of the white-collar crimes of the church as the most publicly presentable option while the opposing side occupied by witch doctors and black magic is strongly protected in entrenched beliefs that are never put on display.

The reality though that public education and the general mindset is trapped between these two lines of religious stupefaction dragging people further down the path of economic impoverishment, does not seem to have dawned on leadership in African societies.

In the absence of inspiring leadership, the steady path to doom in practical and mental development has become a household reality and a way of life in almost all segments of African societies.

* * * * *

Chapter 7

Conclusion with Projections and Recommendations

The ordinary folk as the inconspicuous victim bearing the brunt of the battle of exploitation raging between the two religious establishments has so far, been easy to identify. While social recognition and the preservation of the privileged status dictated by fear and awe (that has defined them from generation to generation) stands at the center of the endeavors of witch doctors and traditional rulers in their capacity as champions of African Traditional Religions, the quest for overnight wealth without hard work drives the activities of the modern white-collar crime of Christian church leaders (bearing the titles of Pastor, Bishop, Vicar, Overseer, Cardinal and Prophet). Quite interesting and worthy of notice is the fact that the original core colonial churches of old – the Catholics, the Baptists and Anglicans – have maintained a distinctive culture that stands out from the new tradition of craze for wealth that is raging madly amongst new generation indigenous African churches. Leaders of the core colonial churches are not known for running private jets. They are not known for holding "Deliverance" rallies or for moving round town with flashy cars and designer dresses. They are hardly identified with visions and miracles in the showmanship trail of African new generation churches. They distinguish themselves by standing in the back row away from the limelight of willful flamboyance.

African new generation churches bearing wild identities in name ("Prayer Warriors", "Guided Missiles Church", "Satan in Trouble Ministry", "Fire for Fire Ministry", etc.)[76] and in their mode of worship are indeed not new to the scene. The concept of mixing elements of the African worshipping traditions (such as drumming, clapping, dancing "into trance" and communication with powers beyond human perception) with church services has long been a characteristic feature of the Cherubim and Seraphim movement. The festive and party atmosphere of loud and noisy worshipping was always combined with the practice of exorcising evil spirits in the state of trance and the weird notion of seeing visions. Time however uncovered the exploitative evolution of this concept of "visionism" and miracle-healing for elevated financial gains by showcasing Jesus-like qualities in individual preachers and self-styled Bishops, Vicars and Overseers. The newfound one-man show churches have now unleashed a new and serious problem on societies that can and should be confronted primarily with political guidance and political intelligence. With politicians consumed in submission to such church leaders patronizing them for blessings and spiritual guidance however, African societies seem lost in a double jeopardy.

NIGERIAN PRESIDENT ON HIS
KNEES BEFORE A PASTOR

The challenge of building a modern society on the basis of scientific education while yet maintaining traditional and cultural institutions that faced the threat of falling into oblivion in the aftermath of colonial administration has been huge enough to confront.

Drawing a line between Occultism and Preserving Cultural Heritage

Far Eastern societies with China and Japan at the forefront have successfully demonstrated to the world that a line can be drawn between modernization and the preservation of cultural and traditional identities. While China thrives on traditional medicine that has been partly subjected to scientific verification, it has succeeded in transferring parts of its ancient practices into universal acceptance in our present day. Acupuncture as a universally accepted method of complementary medical treatment is now a household phenomenon. Japan has succeeded in preserving ancient shrines and other traditional institutions with utmost reverence and yet not allowed such elements to play pervasive roles in the shaping of daily lives amongst the ordinary folks.

India and Brazil are also outstanding examples in two different continents, of countries that have permitted and even deliberately promoted the preservation of cultural and traditional religious practices without negating the importance of science and realistic, rational and progressive practices. While Umbanda, Quimbanda and Candomble are practiced freely in Brazil, the nation does not negate the development and sustenance of an academic tradition and the consolidation of a scientific community to oversee the growth of a parallel life of rational perception for the benefit of Believers and Non-Believers. Like Brazil, India lives a predominantly Hindu life with the parallel growth of a different world in superstition thriving in talisman and beliefs in gods and spirits. Yet science, academics and a parallel life in discerning rational perception is not negated. Today Indian Software programming experts are hotly sought after in western countries. The intermediate result is two countries with a sound and independent base in different branches of scientific exploration.

Pan-Africanism

Unfortunately however, African societies do not seem to seek to preserve pre-colonial traditional, cultural, religious and political institutions and practices as relics of history and move forward. No. In a complex mix of post-colonial complacency and self-importance partly informed by contradictions in the scientific and religious teachings introduced by the white man, Black Africa now seems immersed in a vicious determination to remain in a self-imposed primordial stalemate. It is the clearest misunderstanding of the principles of Pan-Africanism that was advocated as a philosophy to represent *"the aggregation of the historical, cultural, spiritual, artistic, scientific and philosophical legacies of Africans from past times to the present. Pan-Africanism as an ethical system traces its origins from ancient times, and promotes values that are the product of the African civilization and the struggles against slavery, racism, colonialism, and neo-colonialism."*[77]

Today, the bid to promote self-confidence amongst Black Africans by emphasizing reliance on core domestic values, now almost seems to be drifting into a state of the blanket denial of weaknesses. This extreme minority group of indigenous intellectuals strives to reject imported values sometimes claiming as lies and colonial manipulation, every visible or highlighted indication of inferiority. It is the ideology pursued by this minority group under the banner of Pan-Africanism that promotes the pervasive presence of traditional institutions.

Rather than being relics of history, pre-colonial traditional rulers seek to play active roles in the business of political leadership by spiritual intimidation. Politicians seek the blessings and assistance of traditional rulers before launching political projects. Traditional rulers are used as intermediaries to communicate with and gain approval ratings from the grassroots in politically expedient times. Such grassroots population having been held in spiritual intimidation by the perceived powers of traditional rulers is usually forthcoming in toeing the lines advocated by traditional institutions as proxies of political interests. In the end, the encouraged growth of academic life in schools and other institutions of learning is overshadowed by teachings in domestic surroundings which generally accept and fear the superiority of spiritual powers over science.

A consolidated domestic community of independent and virile scientists is thus conspicuously missing in the African equation. The picture that meets the eyes is a community of scientists that is yet struggling to grasp the essence of science and technology in its generally accepted universality. This is compounded by the fact that this community is hardly encouraged and financed by political authority. In the end, the prevalent status is an underfunded class of scientists characterized by a shortage of equipment for experiments to say the least of inventions. Questions also abound on how far-reaching the belief of the African scientist in the science that he practices weighs against his belief in the assisting might of the spirit of the gods and ancestors. The hypothetical imagination that an African scientist after achieving a major feat in his chosen profession ends up performing thanksgiving at a shrine by way of sacrifices to the gods and spirits or ends up before a pastor who may have foretold his achievements in visions will come as no surprise to the discerning mind. The result is that the impact of science in Black Africa is scarcely felt in any area of public life where growth potentials abound in the continent.

Agriculture remains unexplored with fertile land all over the continent. Animal husbandry is yet in a very limited scope. Forward movement is largely based on imported technology from other continents. Asian countries that were subjected to the same colonial oppression suffered by Black Africa now stand out as the guideposts for cheaper credible import commodities produced by these erstwhile comrades in captivity.

The construction sector remains riddled with manual labor in a world progressing in technology. Chinese scientists cultivated in a society that has a strong record of traditional religious beliefs, have shown to the world how science can be advanced by taking example not from the spirit world but from progressive western technology. Today, labor forces for basic technology in the construction and agricultural sector are imported into several African countries from China. Some slots in the educational sector are occupied by Indian labor forces. Crucial positions in oil exploration are occupied by the Americans and Europeans. Pseudo space technology investments are outsourced to China. Yet the African revels in his growing sense of spiritual devotion to the gods and the spirits and the power of Jesus Christ.

"Herbalism" and Natural Medicine

The concept of *Herbalism* was coined from the natural life of ancestral Africans who knew no injections, tablets, X-Ray or medical surgery. It derives from the lives of primordial Africans who maintained a medical life dependent on herbal products for the treatment of ailments. With topographical fertility, Africa is home to a vast array of herbal varieties that ancestral fathers exploited and passed on from generation to generation.

One of the dark sides of colonial intrusion in Africa is arguably the disruption of this established system of hereditary one-way communication between generations. The introduction of western education no doubt served as a distraction from the continuation of this transfer of cultural heritage. Somewhere down the line, a generation or two emerged that is or are less interested in knowing or preserving such hereditary traditional skills of using herbal mixes for medical purposes having learnt about the western alternatives that are said to be largely superior in several ramifications. In fact, the population of Africans with knowledge of the right herbs and herbal mixture to serve the right purposes has shrunk dramatically through several generations. For some reasons however, the average African is obviously unable to draw the bold, thick line separating herbal medicine from witchcraft and sorcery.

The reason is clear. From the start of time, herbal medicine has always been practiced by self-proclaimed clairvoyant healers and media of the spirit world. While there is a basic trust in the chemical composition of herbal combinations for ailments that were properly treated in ancient times before the emergence of colonial intrusion, witch doctors never relented in claiming credit for such feats. They often attributed such credits to their own power of clairvoyance. In the end, the successful healing of ailments through herbal combinations was sold to the discerning mind as a skill derived from clairvoyance and witchcraft. It is therefore all too natural that the common folk is consumed in a basic dose of confusion figuring out this **bold, thick** line distinguishing *witchcraft* from *herbalism* even though the line appears in his mind as **thin** and **fine** if not outright blurred or non-existent.

Today, while other progressive countries recognize this bold, thick line and advance the scientific recognition of traditional medicine as complementary medical treatment, the African witch doctor continues to encourage the popular belief in his own extraordinary status as the holder of the key to parallel medical practice based on his supernatural powers. To compound an already complex and confusing situation, the self-proclaimed *visionists* of Jesus Christ also work hard to encourage belief and trust in the power of prayer and fasting as the ultimate path to redemption from all illnesses. Herbal treatment offered by the self-proclaimed witch doctors is thus declared as evil and ungodly without much ado.

As already indicated above, countries such as India, Pakistan, Bangladesh, South Korea, Malaysia, Indonesia etc. started a political life of national independence very much like every other African country that was released into independence from colonial captivity, by the European colonial powers sometime in the 20th century. Like all Black African countries, they were all traditional societies and agriculture-based economies. Belief in spirits and gods are also phenomena that were and are not unknown to these countries.

Today, many of these countries have grown into industrial economies caring for their traditional identities only as a footnote in contemporary appearance. Black Africa has barely moved forward. The standard of education has dropped enormously and significantly almost across the board. The standard of living hardly stands out for comparison on the international scale. But how earnestly has the question been asked "Where are things going wrong?"

Stretches of forest areas are abandoned in Africa to the fear of spiritual affliction. Till the present moment in the 21st century, there are still vast stretches of dark forest areas in several African societies that many indigenous folks are too afraid to step into. Such fears do not derive from scary wild animals. No. The folks simply fear the regency of evil spirits in such territories. Witch doctors take advantage of such fears to move in and out of such abandoned areas fueling the fear that no 'ordinary' person can go in there. In fact, ordinary persons include scientists. There is hardly any government support in such instances to allay popular fear by encouraging scientific explorations into such dreaded territories to assure the ordinary folks that there is actually nothing in such forest areas to be afraid of. Indeed, government officials and scientists themselves are products of such regimes of spiritual fears and frights much like the ordinary folks.

As already mentioned above, pawpaw trees are abandoned as soon as any witch doctor in the neighborhood declares them a coven of nocturnal conferences held by witches and wizards. Juicy and healthy fruits grow from them and are allowed to waste away for fear of being afflicted by the toxic and invisible taste of witchcraft while Latin American countries like Brazil, Costa Rica or Nicaragua comfortably export less qualitative brands of the pawpaw fruits to Europe and other countries for hard currencies in foreign trade.

Specific brand of trees are abandoned and in some cases turned into sites of worships as soon as they are declared covens for spiritual conventions or as holding supernatural powers of any sort. Witch doctors and shamans turn them into sites for animal sacrifices where the decapitated remains of cats, dogs and fowls are found in the break of day. Such trees remain untouched and unchecked for safety control. One good example is the vast iroko tree – a massive tree with a unique and intimidating size – widely believed by native Africans to be a witchcraft-related object. This tree often grows uncontrolled in public areas with no government authority daring to consider trimming its spreading branches for public safety or controlling it for vegetational health to ensure its stability for public safety as well.

On November 11, 2012, one of such iroko trees estimated to have existed for 200 years at the market square of a Nigerian village (the rural Ifite-Dunu in the Eastern Nigerian state of Anambra) finally fell without external impact. No one had cared for it all the 200 years of its existence. Two persons in its path did not have enough time to scramble to safety. They were taken to their early graves. The tree had been abandoned by the Dunukofia Local Government Authority to public worship and reverence.

"The Iroko tree was said to be the abode of the goddess of sands (Ajani), while its leaves and roots were reported to help fertility and quick delivery of babies." The writer Syvanus Eze reported in a Nigerian newspaper.[78]

In an instant reaction, one eyewitness was quoted as saying:

"It is a miracle; the collapsed Iroko tree is not for nothing. The elders of the town will consult oracles to unveil the cause"[78]

It was of course, party time for the rural witch doctors and spiritual media of this remote village of Ifite-Dunu. The high priests and relevant forces did not wait too long to swing into action.

"The Ajani Chief Priest, who preferred anonymity, said he had consulted oracles, adding that the goddess had given him permission to cut down other old trees at its abode in the market."[78] and thus assumed without much ado, what should ordinarily have been the duty of municipal authorities.

Indeed, while municipal administrations in Europe and other continents routinely keep track of trees and other vegetations in public areas for the purpose of controlling potential hazards to the public, this example of Dunukofia Local Government in Eastern Nigeria shows the helplessness of government authorities in their submission to popular beliefs. It is not uncommon in European cities to find road blocks that are temporarily mounted for a few hours in open streets and the highways for municipal government workers to trim branches of trees and even cut down trees that are potentially hazardous to public safety before any havoc is wreaked. In many African communities though, the situation is routinely different. Elected government officials submit to the fear of gods and spirits and leave some hazardous trees to the fates decided by self-styled clairvoyant high priests and witch doctors. The role of government as a custodian of public safety in such cases is thus outsourced to Chief Priests without much ado. Occasional outcomes are fatalities and costs to human lives as our example has shown.

Cases of fellow human beings being declared as outcasts and stigmatized as witches have been treated above. There are countless examples of the influence of superstitious beliefs on social behavior that political instances adopt and cement in society as social norms.

It is yet a matter of grievous regrets that Africa today, is still struggling to find the rightful places for its traditional institutions and spiritual inclinations in a world driven by rational calculations and progressive practices. The analyst is faced with an almost compelling urge to assume that a completely new generation of Africans will be required to sweep the system clean. Unfortunately and to the disappointment of the analysts however, younger generations come up and are even more corrupt and either too superstitious or Jesus-inclined or both, to show the continent the correct path to uplifting the common people into a path of rational perception.

While the benefits of religious beliefs and practices can and should never be de-emphasized, the clear saturation of social consciousness in many African societies with the notion of religion and spiritism as pillars of redemption to the point of fraudulent exploitation is a phenomenon that should not be ignored through political indifference. As in many aspects of societal development and advancement, this too is an area in which Africa is generally still struggling to strike a healthy balance for future generations. It is undisputable that our contemporary world is immersed in the dictates of technological advancement to improve the day-to-day life of ordinary folks. Nowhere in this forward-moving world however, has any society witnessed social and economic upliftment through the powers of any religion or traditional superstitious beliefs and practices. The unfortunate truth is that the few societies of this world in which superstition and religion dominate the daily life of the common man, are fraught with an extremely low level of affluence and life on the fringes as opposed to societies in which religion and superstition play lesser roles. The peasant folks of Haiti, the slums of Brazil and other Latin-American communities and a vast section of the African continent will stand out as distinctive examples in this regard.

Projections for the future

It is therefore compelling to ask the ultimate question: "Which way out?" Philosophers and sages will ordinarily posit that a problem is half-solved when the problem itself is identified. It would therefore implicitly suggest that the most natural thing to do would be the simple reversal of the elements of the same problem. In other words, the solution is almost always entrenched in the problem itself. Unfortunately however, problems affecting individual persons are hardly solved in simplistic equations and inferences to say the least of a crucial problem plaguing an entire continent over centuries. To assume therefore that a mere paradigm shift from beliefs and religious practices would reverse the fortunes of Africa would be as simplistic as it will be foolhardy in its entirety. Beliefs and religion are inherent fundamental attributes of human nature that can hardly be changed. They are elements of social life that will accompany man to the end of time as long as questions abound on creation and existence. They fill the natural gap that marks man's inherent attribute of naïveté and hunger for stupefaction.

The arrest and control of the spiritual excesses by self-imposed "Men of God" and "Men of the spirit world" in their reckless and wanton exploitation of this natural weakness will mark a crucial step forward in the quest to redeem Africa from its own sins.

While science and technology are yet unable to provide answers to crucial questions on being and existence, they have come a long way in unearthing the simplicity of contents concealed in phenomena that mankind had hitherto believed through the ages, to be complex and beyond the reach of human perception. Today for example, space exploration is waiting to be taken to the next level of casual travels and vacationing. Science and technology have so far, defied the reverence attached to the heavens as the throne of God's Kingdom exposing physical heaven to be nothing beyond clouds and the loss of gravity. There is no use asking where the clouds and the force of gravity come from as they form a package of several unanswered questions in being and existence. Speculative answers based on suppositions will only further heighten the theory of God and Devil as the world already knows.

Alongside these developments is the transformation of religions. The Christian religion that once perceived of rulers as representatives of God, punished criticism of Kings as blasphemy, hunt down and executed critical minds that were branded as witches for being politically critical is today, more mundane and closer to the people thanks to the scientific simplification of common facts. Inquisition is no more. Books are no longer burned. Yet the same religion continues to exist and play a laudable crucial role in unifying people and societies. Except for Ireland in which the politicized elements of the Christian religion have translated into feud and factional fighting, the

Christian religion has largely played and continues to play vital roles in countries all over the world.

While Islam is currently struggling with the concept of interpretation to determine the dominant version of Islam that should be more acceptable to the whole world, it too has come a long way in the path of transformation. Whichever way developments in Islam are viewed, its teachings remain a far cry from the practice of spiritism and superstition that is plaguing peasant communities into collective stupefaction.

In the perverse practice of Christianity, Africans do not regard political leaders as representatives of God as was done in medieval Europe. In its place, Pastors and Preachers are referred to as the "Men of God" with the 'holier than thou' attributes inadvertently leaving the members of congregations as mere followers of the preacher men rather than equally being 'men of God' like the preachers themselves. This hierarchical differentiation automatically defines the inherent and natural human lust for power with the positioning of the lords and those that are lorded over. Yet the followers of visionists and the fraudulent 'Men of God' do not understand that these 'lords' are as human as they themselves are.

Christianity in technologically and democratically advanced societies has truly come a long way. The conclusion of the Second World War in 1945 ushered in the latest round of bitter political reckoning with the Catholic Church for its policy of political appeasement directed at dictators across the board. The issue was confronted and exhaustively explicated by both sides to the controversy. The church transformed in a continuous process and sought to focus more on its inherent duties of working for the good of mankind.

In today's Europe, churches generally stand out for humanitarian activities and commitments. Churches run hospitals, kindergartens, schools, old people's homes, homeless people's homes, eateries for the homeless and temporary winter sanctuaries for homeless and helpless people, etc. All these establishments are run at affordable costs and often free-of-charge for the underprivileged victims.

In Sub-Saharan Africa however, no one learns from the historical past of churches in the countries that brought the religion to Africa in the first place. On the contrary, a section of Black Africans simply claim to have overtaken the colonial owners of the Christian religion spiritually. Rather than running institutions to help the underprivileged masses that litter every African street in abundance, African church leaders build universities that only the rich and privileged can afford. They compete with themselves counting the number of private jets they own for their private use, lavish money on luxury churches, build private luxury homes, wear luxury clothes and simply seem to scorn and mock the poor peasant followers with disdain. In fact, not long ago, I stumbled onto a Nigerian pastor seeking to defend this phenomenon in an online forum. The man who simply called himself Pastor Christopher said:

"We are in an era of prosperity. God said through prosperity shall his kingdom be spread abroad. How can you spread the Gospel to (a place like) China on foot (without airplanes)?" he asked.[79]

Nowhere else in the world do people need affordable healthcare, education and countless public amenities than in Africa. Yet, there is nowhere else in the world where church leaders are so rich and immersed in "Pastorpreneurship" than in Africa. They invest their ill-gotten money in projects to multiply their wealth and never for the good of the sufferers.

Supposed witches are wrongly stigmatized and sometimes physically, emotionally and mentally abused in places of worship. A clear competition rages between witch doctors and self-ordained men of God with the setting getting ever more inhuman and criminal.

In a nutshell, Africa today shows many elements of the early centuries of the civilized world that have long been confined to the dustbin of history. In fact, these dark days in the history of the church are even taken one step further by the Africans through the exploitation of the poor masses who badly need all imaginable help. The claim that Africa is ways ahead of the rest of the world in spiritual development could not be more foolish and self-stupefying.

There is no doubt that forward movement under such socio-political circumstances will always be an uphill task. Yet there is light at the end of the tunnel.

Africa today is no longer what it was three decades ago. No matter how late it has started, the wind of change is now finding its way to the direction of Africa in a slow velocity. How much of a laughing stock in the international community Africa has become is not lost on the new generation of African intellectuals. This segment of the African society that has largely struggled with very limited material resources to ascend to a level of intellectual growth that best qualifies many only as pseudo-intellectuals, has nonetheless taken up the challenge of seeing Africa jump on the ascending ramp of general development. These are intellectuals that have successfully made the best of a very bad situation amid educational infrastructures that have dilapidated steadily since the days of independence from colonialism. Complementing this category is the class of African intellectuals like Kofi Anan of Ghana, Ngozi Okonjo-Iweala of Nigeria and the late Wangari Maathai of Kenya who did not only enjoy the privilege of quality education in countries that could afford them far outside Africa but also served the global community at the highest possible level for practical experiences. The mix of these two classes of intellectuals is now slowly but steadily ushering in the wind of change that is obviously sending preliminary waves sweeping through the continent.

On top of this, Africa is presently the last standing expandable market for international trade. The availability of a huge raw material reserve poses a huge investment and development potential that will implicitly translate and is probably already translating into growth opportunities for the economies of individual African countries. The struggle for dominance and supremacy by competing economic powers (China, USA and Europe) will offer Africa a crucial opportunity to partake in the process of dictating trade terms. In fact, the sinister opportunity of even playing one party against the other stares Africa in the face. It is a future that portends a sharp departure from the days of purely unilateral dictation of trade terms to the perpetual detriment of sick man Africa. Like China, African countries will be faced with the golden opportunity of copying, stealing and indigenizing foreign technology with ingenious smartness. How well this opportunity will be recognized and utilized however, will be a different ballgame altogether.

Development potentials do indeed, look rosy for African leaders and their folks. Competing political indices between individual African countries are also triggering developmental reactions that will leave the present momentum almost unstoppable.

Today, the notion of free and fair election of political leaders in constitutional democracies is knocking on Africa's doors under the leadership of the small state of Ghana. For the first time in the history of Black Africa, Ghana showed to the world that a ruling political party can be defeated in free and fair elections with the ruling party quitting the scene quietly without shedding blood to hang on to power. Today, other countries are showing the determination to follow suit.

The resultant sense of shame felt by bigger nations such as Nigeria who had long imposed on itself the title of "Giant of Africa" while continuing to wallow in corruption and inefficiency is now posing a different challenge in free-flowing dynamics. The gauntlet has been thrown down by little Ghana and other countries are slowly but steadily picking it up to emulate a path destined for greatness.

For more than twenty years, little Ghana has been enjoying uninterrupted power supply – an uncharacteristic feat that no one expected to happen so soon in any sub-Saharan African state. Countries with better and more voluminous resources that however made less out of their rosy situations are now in shame. Once again, Ghana is playing a pioneering role.

The same applies to the small South African state of Botswana that has equally earned itself a reputation as a shining beam of democracy and economic growth in Africa. Unlike the big brother Nigeria which discovered oil even before independence in 1960, Botswana discovered diamonds in 1972. Oil means to the Nigerian export economy what diamonds mean to Botswanan foreign trade. Unlike Nigeria however, little Botswana has ensured the diversification of economic resources that even though diamond accounts for 80% of export earnings, it makes up just 50% of government revenue. Today, according to expert projection, *"Botswana, a nation approximately the size of Texas, is expected to realize continued GDP growth and will converge with the global economic leaders per capita GDP in approximately 26 years – by 2037"*[80]

The prevalent moral state of affairs in Black Africa today is one that sees the would-be weaker entities growing strong enough to shine their lights to illuminate the path of progress for the presumably stronger forces.

To underscore this fact, the first ever black President to rule the world's most influential country Barrack Obama of the United States of America rightly singled out Ghana for his first and (thus far) only visit to Black Africa. Ever since, a ripple effect has been triggered within the continent! The sense of shame that President Barrack Obama deliberately exacerbated with his speech in Ghana could not have hit the neighboring country Nigeria any harder.

*"No country is going to create wealth if its leaders exploit the economy to enrich themselves, or police can be bought off by drug traffickers. No business wants to invest in a place where the government skims 20 percent off the top, or the head of the **Port Authority** is corrupt. No person wants to live in a society where the rule of law gives way to the rule of brutality and bribery."*[81]

Indeed there is hardly any Sub-Saharan African country in which the government is so entrenched in skimming off a huge percentage of contract sums from investors than Nigeria. There is hardly any other Black African country in which corruption by the heads of the Port Authority is as rampant as in Nigeria. Indeed many discerning Nigerian youths and intellectuals were highly thankful to President Obama for this blunt and hardly veiled push and slap on the face of evil. Indeed before him, the American Secretary of State Mrs. Hillary Clinton had visited Nigeria and told the corrupt leaders in no unmistakable terms that the *"failure of government at the federal, state and local level"* was responsible for a state of desperate poverty despite abundant wealth and resources.[82]

With the message and challenge now getting through in clear terms, politicians are beginning to show a stronger determination to do better than ever before. With the United Nation's Millennium Development Goals (MDG) aimed at poverty eradication, even the most unintelligent of leaders are shown the way that development should be planned. Agenda 20:2020, etc. is one such reaction that has followed in Nigeria.

Technologically advanced South Africa handed over by the Apartheid whites to impoverished blacks has managed to avoid the depletion of the development and resources met on the ground. Technology is now being exported to other Black African countries in many ramifications.

Taking Nigeria as a prototype of countries feeling the ripple effect of Ghana's surge, a few governments in the periphery are today seen to be increasingly living up to the challenges of ruling for the folks. Development at the grassroots now seems to be taking hold of rulership awareness.

In a nutshell, Sub-Saharan Africa of the next two to three decades (i.e. 2033 to 2043) will strongly differ from Africa of the year 2013. Infrastructural advancement will take a remarkable turn for the better. Welfare indexes will take a northward turn and the standard of living will usher in more smiling faces. In other words, today's trademark pothole and dusty roads, comatose power and water supply systems will see a remarkable improvement as several countries now pour immense resources into registering a forward movement in this sector. Other crucial infrastructures such as hospital, educational, road-safety facilities etc. will get the knock-on effect and pick up a measured leap from their current torturing comfort on the sick-man's bed. School laboratories that have consistently suffered from poor power supply and lack of instruments are then likely to move back to where they were shortly after independence from the colonial years. Rather than being the death traps that many of them currently are, hospitals are likely to advance to life-saving establishments when power and water supply improves. Days will be ushered in, in which patients no longer die of Diabetes or minor road accident injuries and women while giving birth in maternity homes.

Recommendations

Unfortunately however, Africa will be faced with the problem of sustaining such giant strides. A balance can hardly be struck between imported and copied development and the non-availability of a virile community of domestic scientists. A society that fails to acquire and utilize the practical know-how of creation and places more emphasis on showcasing the end-product of hard labor without the underlying methodical process will run into trouble as time progresses.

Shortage of the infrastructures of creation in Africa will mean that societies will acquire good roads and improved facilities in many areas that they will be unable to maintain and sustain over time. The failure of political leadership to invest strongly in education and academic development will most certainly mark a date of expiration for infrastructural gains. With a track record of neglecting structural maintenance, the duty of sustaining development and growth in Africa will rest with pressure groups and the media to set the proper agenda for a forward movement when progress finally comes.

One major reason the desire to sustain Africa's infrastructural development will surely hit rock bottom – when it finally arrives – is the formidable and widespread belief in spirits, gods, witchcraft and the powers of the Holy Ghost.

Belief, which – as can be understood in the foregoing analysis – is presently holding Africa hostage in intellectual captivity! Getting the continent away from this self-destructing bondage will require the growth of science and a focused political policy aimed at encouraging independent thinking.

A society without an independent scientific base will have no clue on handling imported technology to say the least of creating its own level of development hardware. To sustain imported technology, foreign technicians and scientists will always be required on the ground for as long as society can afford their expenses. If the society however sinks deeper in the quest of the individual, to get rich overnight by patronizing the powers of gods and spirits, the time required for learning contents from foreign technicians and scientists, will be spent seeking the help of gods and spirits to facilitate stealing and encouraging the foreign technicians and scientists to steal as well. In the end, roads constructed will suffer rapid losses of quality because there will be no local resources to fix them. Hospitals will lose equipment when there is no means of producing them with local expertise. School laboratories will lose materials because the money has been stolen and the quality of education pays the price, etc. etc.

Today's political leadership status in Africa is one that exemplifies religion and beliefs as a fashionable way of living a healthy life. This is absolutely nothing wrong if all other peripheral conditions were put in place! Frequent calls on people by

African politicians, to join in prayers to solve the overwhelming problems confronting their societies, have oftentimes served to disarm the critical masses from seeking accountability from their leaders since all powers are perceived to lie with God who did not campaign for any political office. Since the leaders are not God, attention is diverted from the leaders as the ultimate authority at whose feet the buck stops. What is left to appeal to is often the abstract phenomenon of the almighty God to guide and move the country forward. This deliberate appeal to faith and functional activation of mass stupefaction has often been described by observers, as a declaration of intellectual and leadership bankruptcy marking a state of leadership helplessness since prayer can never be sold as a formal government policy. Unfortunately, this is not an uncommon feature of African leadership appeal.

The promotion of science by creating awards for excellence in scientific research and inventions as one means of emphasizing government's determination to spread the popular embrace of academic orientation and upliftment of rational and objective reasoning is a method that African leaders are yet to discover. Yet, year in, year out, they witness the global Nobel Prize for academic achievements as an example of what can be done to promote one's own domestic growth in academic explorations. On the contrary, there is a growing trend of hiking annual budgetary allocations for refreshment and personal comfort in government houses and building of palatial edifices for political leaders. African leaders hardly ask themselves why nothing is ever heard of African science and scientists when the annual Nobel Prize award for science is announced in its cyclical routine.

The duty of governments to initiate and lead scientific explorations into so-called 'evil forests' that litter several rural communities in Africa in a bid to help alleviate the awesome fear of such forests in the minds of local population, does not occur to African leaders. On the contrary, deliberate efforts are made to keep citizens in a state of emotional submission to abstract and invisible powers that can be instrumentally appealed to when the need arises. After all, if the President of a country can fall on his knees before a pastor in front of cameras and microphones seeking divine assistance in governance, who is the ordinary man not to ask for "pastorpreneural" blessings for private problems? In the end, African leaders negate their duties of fighting the white-collar crimes perpetrated by church leaders, who then feel free to act with impunity. Leaders seem blind to the failure if not outright refusal of churches and self-styled holy men to help the folks out of poverty with humanitarian projects. Instead, absolute competition is on course between church leaders to own the highest number of private jets for the spread of God's words to aliens in space.

Elevating government awareness in this field may mark a crucial step out of Africa's diabolical entrapment. Gains in this respect will be further strengthened if the issue of traditional rulers is addressed with a view to finding formal constitutional solutions.

Assigning the constitutional roles of running or playing leading roles in Ministries of Culture to traditional rulers at peripheral levels with a clear mandate to cooperate closely with a special institute of state-sponsored scientists and researchers of the academia may be a crucial step in the right direction. The commitment of traditional rulers in their constitutional capacities as functionaries of Ministries of Culture, to close cooperation with science will then seek to pursue the ultimate objective of largely re-enacting elements of alternative medicine taken from herbal and other natural products that were known to the ancestors. It will also seek to systematize the historical aspects of traditional institutions that should be elevated as monumental and protection-worthy relics of the past in the strict sense of the word. A project that will no doubt, require intensive brainstorming for the creation of workable details.

In the end, the creation of traditional clinics focused on the healing of ailments the traditional way in complementation of academic medicine with close monitoring and setting of standards by administrative processes and emulation of the Brazilian model of the Umbanda, Quimbanda and Cadomble clinics will be a highly welcome development. A process will thus be set in motion to de-emphasize the notion of witchcraft that has so badly enveloped the masses in a suffocating trap of wanton submission. Efforts will then be geared towards the gradual phasing out and eradication of this socially useless and unproductive but pervasive and captivating phenomenon of the folly of man. The outcome of rediscovering potentially useful products of natural medicine that are easily affordable and even within the do-it-yourself range of the peasant village dweller in the rural setting will no longer be an uncommon phenomenon. The spread and institutionalization of the concept over time will be realized through the involvement of private investors and controllable commercial interests. Local forests will thus be exploited in an optimized manner that should seek to strike an ecological balance while man makes a quantum leap into a state of the unison with nature that will be taken to another level. A level of reduced fear and less diabolical fairy tales! The fear of witches, spirits and gods will be naturally demystified and people may slowly begin to act with more confidence in their power to control their own environments.

Committed government machineries with the altruistic policy of sanitizing society and rural communities, will surely seek to work out constitutional feasibility details for the attainment of these redeeming goals. Until progress is made on this front, Africa will continue to wallow in the ugly swamp of collective mental and intellectual deprivation, leaving it at the mercy of spiritual conmen and smart religious exploitation. There will be no ESCAPE from the self-imposed DIABOLICAL ENTRAPMENT!

* * * * *

Footnotes

1. Source: www.heroesofhistory.com/page58.html

2. Source: Newspaper article: "Alleged membership of witchcraft cult: 95-yr-old beaten to death, children dehumanized" Vanguard newspaper October 27, 2011 (Nigeria)

3. Source: Online Dictionary "Merriam Webster"

4. Source: Online Encyclopaedia "Wikipedia" – Article: "Thunderstorm"

5. Source: Online Encyclopaedia "Wikipedia" – On Stephen Hawking

6. Source: www.guardian.co.uk/science/2011/may/15/ stephen-hawking-interview-there-is-no-heaven

7. Source: www.guardian.co.uk/science/2011/may/15/ stephen-hawking-interview-there-is-no-heaven

8. Source: Chris LaRocco and Blair Rothstein: THE BIG BANG: It sure was BIG!! www.umich.edu/~gs265/ bigbang.htm

9. Source: www.exposingsatanism.org

10. Viewer's comment: 40Pacino in www.youtube.com/ watch?v=2TbEitVbyF0

11. Source: www.history.com/topics/halloween

12. Source: www.history.com/topics/halloween

13. Source: Online Dictionary: www.wordreference.com

14. Source: www.history.com/topics/halloween

15. Source: www.youtube.com/watch?v=yDU8g72_rXQ

16. Source: www.dw.de/aberglaube-in-europa/a-5879763-1

17. Source: Wikipedia

18. Source: www.polnische-hochzeit.de

19. Source: www.netimage.pl

20. Source: Polish Magazine "Samo Zycie" Issue No. 23, published in Dortmund, Germany

21. Source: www.netzeitung.de/vermischtes/372463.html

22. Source: www.netzeitung.de/vermischtes/372463.html

23. Source: www.dw.de/aberglaube-in-europa/a-5879763-1

24. Source: www.dw.de/aberglaube-in-europa/a-5879763-1

25. Source: www.dw.de/aberglaube-in-europa/a-5879763-1

26. Source: www.dw.de/aberglaube-in-europa/a-5879763-1

27. Source: www.wordreference.com

28. Source: Wikipedia

29. Source: Wikipedia

30. Source: Wikipedia

31. Source: "You Forever" by Tuesday Lobsang Rampa

32. Source: Article by Christian Purefoy writing for CNN: "edition.cnn.com/2010/WORLD/africa/08/25/nigeria.child.witches/index.html"

33. Source: VANGUARD newspaper (Nigeria), June 04, 2011, Article "Witchcraft: Govt. should sign the Child Rights Act" by Florence Amagiya

34. Source: THE NATION newspaper (Nigeria), December 10, 2011, Report "For Pa Oboh, life begins at 98 with a new bride" by Olukayode Thomas.

35. Source: "Times of India" quoted in "Sabah" (Turkey), 28 Dec. 2010 & "TIME Newsfeed" October 18, 2012

36. Source: www.ncbi.nlm.nih.gov/pmc/articles/PMC1174728/

37. Source: http://psychologyafrica.com/2009/03/alzheimers-a-white-mans-disease/

38. Source: Source: Sigmund Freud, "The Interpretation of Dreams", 1900 (Wikipedia)

39. Source: http://psychology.about.com/od/statesofconsciousness/p/dream-theories.html

40. Source: Dictionary.com

41. Source: www.thekeep.org/~kunoichi/kunoichi/themestream/egypt_humansacrifice.html

42. Source: http://en.wikipedia.org/wiki/Human_sacrifice

43. Source: http://en.wikipedia.org/wiki/Human_sacrifice

44. Source: The Telegraph, January 07, 2010 (www.telegraph.co.uk/news/worldnews/africaandindianocean/uganda/6944292/Human-sacrifices-on-the-rise-in-Uganda-as-witch-doctors-admit-to-rituals.html)

45. Nigeria's "Newswatch" of August 16, 2004, "The Confessions of Okija Shrine Priests" by Chris Ajaero (www.newswatchngr.com/editorial/prime/Cover/10816185839.htm)

46. Source: www.howardforums.com/printthread.php?t=427591

47. Source: http://nigeriantimes.blogspot.de/2011/03/warning-strange-happenings-in-nigeria.html

48. Source: www.nigeriavillagesquare.com/forum/archive/index.php/t-33289.html

49. Source: http://ihuanedo.ning.com/profiles/blogs/the-resurgence-of-ayelala-in?xg_source=msg_mes_network

50. Source: www.nigerianobservernews.com/28112010/28112010/sundayobserver/5.html

51. Source: www.vanguardngr.com/2012/09/man-shoots-son-dead-in-failed-bullet-proof-charm-test-2/

52. Source: Wikipedia

53. Source: Wikipedia

54. Source: www.infoplease.com - "Kingdoms and Monarchs of the World"

55. Source: Wikipedia

56. Source: www.icpsr.org.ma/?Page=showInstitute&InstituteID=NIFOPR123&CountryID=Nigeria

57. Source: www.huffingtonpost.com/2009/11/29/10000-albinos-in-hiding-a_n_372976.html

58. Source: www.theworld.org/2010/06/the-murder-of-albinos-in-tanzania/

59. Source: http://www.welt.de/dieweltbewegen/article13743903/Das-Dorf-aus-dem-die-Aids-Seuche-kam.html

60. Source: http://en.wikipedia.org/wiki/Opium_of_the_people

61. Source: The Nigerian "SUN", January 20, 2012: "Horror in Oshogbo"

62. Source: Nigerian "Vanguard", April 10, 2012 ""Prophet" arraigned over N600,000 fraud"

63. Source: Nigerian "Vanguard", June 20, 2012, "Police arrest 7 fake pastors over sham deliverance

64. Source: www.ghanaweb.com/GhanaHomePage/ NewsArchive/artikel.php?ID=208920

65. Source: Wikipedia "Stockholm syndrome"

66. Source: May 24, 2006 Edition 1, © 2006 Post & Independent Online (Pty) Ltd, South Africa

67. Source: Mail Online November 02, 2010, www. dailymail.co.uk, "Jesus was HIV-positive"

68. Source: www.dailymail.co.uk/news/article-2220833/ Laughing-private-jet—93m-pastor-accused-exploiting-British-worshippers.html

69. Source: www.dailymail.co.uk/news/article-2220833/ Laughing-private-jet—93m-pastor-accused-exploiting-British-worshippers.html and www.nairaland. com/899018/dominion-air-bishop-david-oyedepo

70. Source: Video link: http://news1.ghananation.com/ video/265645-nigerian-bishop-david-oyedepo-slaps-girl-accused-of-witchcraft-during-deliverance-video. html

71. Source: http://newnigerianpolitics.com/2011/12/20/ bishop-david-oyedepo-caught-on-video-assaultingabusing-a-child-in-his-church/

72. Source: www.ascology.com "Holy Slap: Suit against Bishop Oyedepo starts Wednesday"

73. Source: www.dailymail.co.uk/news/article-2220833/ Laughing-private-jet—93m-pastor-accused-exploiting-British-worshippers.html

74. Source: www.ibtimes.com/6-deaths-british-churches-claim-cure-hiv-prayer-375144

75. Source: www.punchng.com/news/jonathan-defends-self-over-church-gift/

76. Source: www.nairaland.com/508429/names-churches-nigeria

77. Source: Wikipedia – Pan-Africanism – quoting "The Politics of Liberation", by Hakim Adi, African Holocaust Society

78. Source: www.tribune.com.ng/index.php/news/50851-200-yr-old-iroko-tree-kills-2-injures-8, Nigerian Tribune, November 14, 2012

79. Source: www.vanguardngr.com/2012/11/private-jets-pastor-bakare-under-fire/

80. Source: www.huffingtonpost.com/nake-m-kamrany/botswana-economic-growth_b_2069226.html

81. Source: www.huffingtonpost.com/2009/07/11/obama-ghana-speech-full-t_n_230009.html

82. Source: www.nytimes.com/2009/08/13/world/africa/13diplo.html

Bibliography

1. Website: Heroes of History (www.heroesofhistory.com)

2. Several issues of the Nigerian newspaper "Vanguard"

3. Online dictionary "Merriam Webster" (www.Merriam-Webster.com)

4. Online Encyclopaedia "Wikipedia"

5. English newspaper "Guardian"

6. Article by Chris LaRocco and Blair Rothstein: "THE BIG BANG: It sure was BIG!" (www.umich.edu)

7. Website: Exposing Satanism (www.exposingsatanism.org)

8. Users' comments on Youtube (www.youtube.com)

9. History website: (www.history.com)

10. Online dictionary "Word Reference" (www. wordreference.com)

11. Website: German World Service Broadcast "Deutsche Welle" (www.dw.de)

12. Website: "Wedding in Poland" (www.polnische-hochzeit.de)

13. Polish website: "Net Image" (www.netimage.pl)

14. Polish magazine "Samo Zycie", issue No. 23, Dortmund, Germany

15. German website: "Net Magazine" (www.netzeitung.de)

16. "You Forever" by Tuesday Lobsang Rampa

17. Article by Christian Purefoy writing for CNN: "Children abused, killed as witches in Nigeria" (edition.cnn.com)

18. Issues of the Nigerian newspaper "The Nation"

19. Turkish newspaper "Sabah" December 28, 2011

20. "TIME Newsfeed" October 18, 2012

21. Website: (www.ncbl.nlm.nih.gov)

22. Article: "Alzheimer's A White man's disease?" by Dr. Jopie de Beer

23. Website: (http://psychology.about.com)

24. Online dictionary: (www.dictionary.com)

25. Website: (www.thekeep.org)

26. Issue of British newspaper: "The Telegraph", January 07, 2010

27. Issue of Nigeria's weekly magazine "Newswatch", August 16, 2004

28. Website: (www.howardforums.com)

29. Website: (http://nigeriantimes.blogspot.de)

30. Website: (www.nigeriavillagesquare.com)

31. Website: (http://ihuanedo.ning.com)

32. Issue of Nigerian newspaper "Nigerian Observer" November 28, 2010

33. Website: (www.infoplease.com)

34. Website: www.icpsr.org.ma

35. Website: www.huffingtonpost.com

36. Website: www.theworld.org

37. Website: www.welt.de

38. Issues of Nigerian newspaper "SUN"

39. Website: www.ghanaweb.com

40. Post & Independent Online (Pty), South Africa, May 24, 2006 Edition

41. Website: www.dailymail.co.uk

42. Website: http://news1.ghananation.com

43. Website: www.newnigerianpolitics.com

44. Website: www.ascology.com

45. Website: www.ibtimes.com

46. Issues of Nigerian newspaper "PUNCH"

47. Issues of Nigerian newspaper "TRIBUNE"

48. Website: www.nairaland.com

49. Website: www.nytimes.com

Annexes

Annex 1: Reuters Report on animist rituals in Nigeria

Sorcerers Nabbed with 50 Bodies, 20 Skulls

LAGOS (Reuters) - Nigerian police have arrested 30 witch-doctors in a raid on fetish shrines in southeast Anambra state where over 50 decomposing bodies and 20 human skulls were discovered, a police spokesman said Thursday.

The heads, genitals and other vital parts of some of the bodies, found in a teak forest in Okija village, had been severed, a sign they may have been killed for ritual.

"We saw more than 50 bodies in various coffins. There were several skulls, some of them really fresh," Anambra police spokesman Kolapo Shofoluwe told Reuters by telephone.

Ritual killing is common in some parts of Nigeria where many people believe they can become instant millionaires by using human organs to make potent charms. Many Nigerians mix traditional religions with Christianity or Islam.

Police said preliminary investigations showed that the people died after the sorcerers engaged them in an animist ritual.

As part of the ritual, the victims pledged their property, including bank accounts, to a deity upon their death, the officer said. Their relations were made to believe they would also die if they refused to give up the property.

"We are looking beyond the deity," Shofoluwe said, adding that at least 20 shrines were raided.

"The priests may have killed the people for ritual, or to obtain their property by false pretence or they may have been running a human parts market," he said.

Shofoluwe quoted a villager who had tipped police off, as saying the sorcerers ate the flesh of some of their victims.

Annex 2: The Confessions of Okija Shrine Priests

By Chris Ajaero
Monday, August 16, 2004

Some of the arrested priests spoke exclusively to Newswatch in their police cells on their role as priests, the people who visit the shrines and the fees charged for consultations

The serene atmosphere that pervades the sleepy and hilly Okija community will in no way give an inkling to the horrors that lie hidden in its thick forest. The once boisterous community which was a haven for people seeking spiritual relief from oppression has suddenly become a ghost town since the police raid of the Ogwugwu Isiula and Ogwugwu Akpu shrines which led to arrest of 39 traditional shrine priests.

The priests who were arrested August 4 allegedly for multiple murder remained defiant as they narrated to Newswatch how they carry out their fetish practices until the police struck.

Felix Ogbaudu, commissioner of police, Anambra State command was happy after that day's successful operation. He exuded the confidence of a tough cop as he paraded the traditional priests of these two notorious shrines in Okija.

Acting on a petition endorsed by Tafa Balogun, inspector-general of police, IGP, Ogbaudu and

Gabriel Haruna, commander of the special anti-robbery squad in the state led a crack team of policemen who raided the Ogwugwu Isiula and Ogwugwu Akpu shrines in Okija. In the process, they recovered 20 human skulls and one fresh corpse in a coffin from the shrines. It was indeed a gory sight as the police displayed the human skulls and corpses some of which were decomposing.

Since this earth-shaking expose of the barbaric acts of the priests in the dreaded Okija shrines, the police have stepped up their investigation to further unravel the mystery behind this shocking discovery. In a bid to dig deep into the mode of operation of the custodians of the Okija shrines, Newswatch visited the evil forest last Monday and later trailed the suspects to the Anambra State police headquarters in Awka where they were being detained. Five of the suspects who spoke to Newswatch confessed how the persons whose skulls were found in the shrines were killed. They claimed that the human skulls and decomposing corpses found in their shrines were not killed for rituals but were the remains of individuals struck dead by the deities for their evil deeds such as lying, greed and oppression of fellow human beings. According to them, when such persons die, their corpses are usually brought to the shrine by their relations because if they failed to do so, they would incur the wrath of the deity which could kill more relations of the deceased. The properties of the deceased acquired through the divination of the deity are also deposited at the shrine.

Edinmuo Ndukwu, one of the priests of Ogwugwu Isiula told Newswatch that the deity demands that persons who want favour from it should always speak the truth and when they tell lies before it, they stand the risk of being struck to death by it. "I would like to state that the philosophy of the Ogwugwu Isiula deity is Eziokwu bu ndu, asi bu onwu, meaning that truth brings life while falsehood leads to death. Therefore, it is the telling of lies by certain persons that leads to their death. If a person swears falsely before the Ogwugwu Isiula deity, it will strike him or her dead," Ndukwu said.

He admitted that the deity could make people rich if they so desire and make such a request but that the priests at the Okija shrines do not use human heads for rituals. Rather, what their clients bring to them are kola and wine. Later on when the deity grants their requests, they would come and express gratitude to the priests in fulfillment of their promises to the deity. Those who fail to fulfill their promises to the deity also stand the risk of being killed by it.

Ndukwu noted that the deity has the power to make a barren woman conceive and bear children. It is also known to have ensured amicable settlement of land disputes when such cases are brought before it. Ndukwu who is a professed idol worshipper wondered why they were being persecuted by the police when there has not been reported incidents of missing persons in Okija in recent times which was traced to the Okija shrines.

Osita Ndu a.k.a. Anwunta (mosquito), son of Ndukwu and another priest of Ogwugwu Isiula deity corroborated his father's position on the issue. Ndu who claimed to be a member of the Anglican Church did not see anything wrong with the skulls and corpses found in the shrines because some of them have been there for ages. He explained that by worshipping idols even when he is a Christian he was obeying the biblical injunction that adherents should "give unto Caesar what is Caesar's and to God what belongs to God." He denied the allegation that they used incantations and magical powers to instruct the deity to strike people dead. According to him, he is merely an errand boy to Okolie Ezike, his grand father and chief priest who has the power to command the deity to kill evil doers. Ezike is more than 100 years old and was not arrested by the police because of his age.

Ndu told Newswatch that he was not touched by the number of corpses that litter the shrine because the practice has been in existence from ancient times and it is a cultural heritage handed down to them by their forefathers. To him, Ogwugwu Isiula is a harbinger of prosperity and offers solutions to the problems of persons who visit it to seek its intervention in their various endeavours in life. Top politicians, businessmen, civil servants, rich and poor people visit the shrines to request the deities to make them succeed in life. When they succeed in life they come back to the shrine to pay homage.

Anthony Okonkwo, secretary Ogwugwu Isiula shrine who is in charge of keeping records of both the dead and other clients of the chief priest told Newswatch that each client pays N580 as consultation fee. Of this amount, N250 is for Kola and hot drinks for the elders while the balance of N330 is shared between the chief priest and the secretary. And whenever the shrine kills somebody, his or her relations will while coming to deposit his corpse in the evil forest, bring one goat, one cock, one hot drink and then the sum of N20,000 to N30,000 will be handed over to the chief priest.

While the Ogwugwu Isiula shrine is noted for prosperity, Ogwugwu Akpu is associated with productivity and fruitfulness. James Obi, 50, one of the priests of the shrine told Newswatch that the deity kills only wicked persons who do not wish their fellow human beings well. Ironically, Obi is a member of the Anglican Church. He, however, believes that idol worshippers are more righteous than some Christians because they do not oppress their neighbours and relations for fear of being killed by the deity. "It is under the traditional religion that people speak the truth as opposed to the church which thrives on falsehood. Many Christians oppress their neighbours and relations. But idol worshippers are upright because the deity does not condone falsehood," he said. He warned that if the deities were destroyed poor people will suffer greatly because rich people will now oppress them with impunity.

But Collins Obi, one of the suspects denied being a priest of the Okija shrine. He claimed that he was arrested in the house of Bartholomew Ndukwu, one of the priests who has been declared wanted by the police. Ndukwu's house is located within the shrine. He said his relationship with the priests of the shrine began two years ago when Obed Igwe, the man whose petition to the IGP led to the raiding of the shrine accused him of duping him of the sum of N600,000. He was later taken to Ogwugwu Akpu shrine by Igwe where they swore an oath not to harm each other.

But Igwe went ahead to report him to Bakassi Boys who arrested him and nearly killed him on February 24, 2002. He escaped death by the whiskers when one of the Bakassi Boys asked them to spare his life because he was not guilty. He was released on bail and asked to pay N100,000. Since he did no have such an amount, Osita Ndukwu and his brother, Bartholomew paid the money on his behalf and since then he has been an errands boy of Bartholomew.

Despite the claim by the suspects that they should not be held responsible for the death of persons whose skulls were found in their shrines the police thinks otherwise. Ogbaudu, the Anambra State police commissioner, told Newswatch that although the suspects had the right to put up any defence, they would have to explain how the skulls of their victims were dismembered from their bodies. "If they were struck dead by the deity, why don't you allow them to get decomposed in the forest, why would somebody go into the forest again, harvest skulls and put in the shrine," he queried.

He also alleged that police investigations have proved that the present custodians of the shrines abuse the practice by using it to intimidate and maim some innocent persons who are perceived enemies of their clients. It was learnt that what some of the priests do is to write the name of such a person on a piece of paper, put gun powder on it, wrap it, and use the cannon to shoot. This is done with incantations and once the gunshot was released, the person whose name was written on the paper would die instantly and the priests will claim he was killed by the shrine.

Ogbaudu believes that the practice as obtained in the past has been adulterated by the present day traditional priests. According to him, somebody phoned him from Abuja last Monday to inform him that he was recently dragged to a shrine where they extorted N800,000 from him for what he knew nothing about. To him, the police would be failing in their responsibility of protecting lives and properties if they permit this type of barbaric practice in the 20th century.

Kolapo Sofoluwe, police public relations officer, Anambra State command, said the 10 registers of victims found in the Okija shrines were being screened to enable the police see how to link them with the corpses and know whether the bodies of prominent Nigerians are among them. The police investigative team is equally considering inviting a pathologist to subject the corpses and skulls to autopsy to establish the actual cause of their death.

The raiding of the shrines has attracted mixed reactions from Nigerians. While some people perceive it as an infringement on the rights of the traditional priests to freedom of worship, others see it as a step in the right direction because the custodians of the shrines were portraying Igbo as primitive. Okechukwu Okani, counsel to the custodians of Ogwugwu Isiula shrine last week threatened to institute a legal action against the police for defiling the shrine thereby infringing on his clients' right to freedom of worship. The South- East Council of Chief Priests, Anambra State chapter is also up in arms against the police. Last Monday the priests warned those who raided the shrines to appease the goddess of Ogwugwu to avert an impending doom. Onuchukwu James Clark, leader of the group, threatened that the chief priests would invoke the spirits of the deities against the raiders if they failed to appease the deities

Already, the priests have begun a seven-day fasting, prayer and hourly incantations to evoke the other deities in the state to fight the cause of the Okija deities. Clark described the invasion of the shrines as a breach of the 1999 constitution, which recognised freedom of religion and association. He also called for the prosecution of Igwe, the police informant whom he accused of not only worshipping the Ogwugwu deity but also practising idolatry at the Lord Simbad Temple which he set up in Amuwo Odofin, Lagos.

The chief priests are very angry with Igwe for what they consider as his act of sabotage.

Igwe himself has become a troubled man. Last week, he called Haruna, the commander who led the team that raided the shrine to complain that his life was being threatened. Police has promised to grant him adequate protection while investigation into the case continues.

As the chief priests of Anambra State attempt to avenge the alleged desecration of the Ogwugwu deities, prominent Nigerians have praised the police for the courage with which they raided the dreaded shrines. Chukwuemeka Odumegwu Ojukwu, Eze Igbo Gburugburu and Ikemba Nnewi welcomed the action. He condemned the practice whereby some persons use the shrines, including the Ogboni and Ekpe societies for political purposes. "The primitiveness exhibited in our society sickens me," he quipped. Ojukwu said that since 1960 when Nigeria gained its independence these kinds of primitive acts have been in existence and nothing has been done to stop them. "It worries me that these are things we as leaders should be thinking of and we are not doing them but bickering," he said.

Chuma Nzeribe, a member of the House of Representatives from Ihiala Federal Constituency of Anambra State, last Wednesday commended the police for their act of courage in fishing out these ugly scenes. "What is reprehensible in this case is the practice of using human remains for idol worship, that is reprehensible, that is ugly, that is un-Christian and no civilised society whatsoever will tolerate such a practice," he said. He, however, noted that there are shrines all over the country and so it would be unfair to create the impression that only Ndigbo have such shrines.

Indeed, many eminent Igbo personalities are worried about the shocking revelations at the Okija shrines. They are miffed that the police was aware of the existence of such shrines all along but did nothing to stop their acts which tend to take the country back to the dark ages.

Newswatch investigations revealed that there are similar shrines in Yoruba, Hausa, Ijaw and Bini, Itshekiri, and other ethnic groups in the country. Some of the dreaded shrines in Nigeria are Ayelala in Ilaje, Ondo State, Somorika in Edo, Iyioji Odekpe of Ogbaru, Habba of Agulu, Ogwugwu Akpo of Ozubulu, Edo of Nnewi and Alaogbaga of Mbaise in Imo state. The bitterness among Igbo elites over the Okija shrine episode explains why Joe Achuzia, secretary general of Ohaneze Ndigbo described the action as calculated at embarrassing the Igbo race.

But last Tuesday the leadership of Ohaneze Ndigbo dissociated itself from the Achuzia's statement. A statement signed by Emmanuel Ajoku, national publicity secretary of Ohaneze, noted that "all the information and allegations contained in the said reports are totally alien to the leadership of Ohaneze and millions of reputable and responsible Ndigbo."

He said: "Ohaneze Ndigbo is a responsible law-abiding organisation totally committed to the modern concepts of democracy and the rule of law. It endorses and recognises the duties and responsibilities of the police in the enforcement of the laws of the land. Ohaneze and millions of law-abiding Ndigbo whose interest and aspirations it represents, will never support any attempt to restrain the police or any other law enforcement agency from carrying out, justly and equitably, its legitimate functions at detecting crimes." The Igbo socio-cultural organisation perceives the Okija discovery as a major tragedy that calls for serious reflections by all right-thinking Nigerians.

Last week, the inspector-general of police received a presidential directive to personally take charge of the on-going investigation into the Okija shrine and he deployed more police detectives for the task. But police authorities said they have not ordered for a clamp down on other shrines similar to the dreaded ones in Okija. Chris Olakpe, deputy commissioner of police and force public relations officer, told Newswatch that the police would only rely on information from members of the public on the existence of such other shrines anywhere in the country, to carry out such action. He said the police does not have knowledge of where such shrines exist.

Indeed, the incident of August 4, has dented the image of Okija community. Although the community has electricity, it is virtually a rural setting. The road leading to Okija is dusty, bumpy and dilapidated and the common mode of transport to the community is motorcycle popularly called Okada.

Since the raiding of the Okija shrines by the police, many men who are indigenes of the area have deserted the community. When Newswatch visited the community last week, it was like a ghost town. The locations of the dreaded Ogwugwu shrines were shadows of their old selves. But the shrines looked quite fearsome as they were in a very thick forest and the skeletons as well as carcasses of human being still littered all over the place. The stench of decomposing corpses in the forest was despicable.

Many indigenes of the community were afraid to speak to the press for fear of harassment by the police. Newswatch, however, learnt that shrines are an important part of the cultural heritage of Okija people. These shrines have been in existence from time immemorial and are passed down from generation to generation. It is the chief priest who acts as an intermediary between the people and the deity. Despite the spread of Christianity to the community, many of its indigenes still believe in the power of the Ogwugwu deity. Although there were no reported cases of missing persons or ritual murders in the area in recent times, a female student of the Madonna University, Okija who spoke to Newswatch on condition of anonymity said such incidents were rampant five years ago when the institution was established.

According to her, many students of the institution who were living off-campus in Okija villages were dying mysteriously without any concrete explanation from their respective landlords as the causes of their death. This compelled Emmanuel Edeh, a Catholic priest and chancellor of the University to direct that the students of the school should no longer live off-campus. They were also warned never to go near the Okija river even if there was no water on campus. This was how cases of mysterious death of students of the university was curbed.

The raiding and arrest of the priests of the Ogwugwu shrines have no doubt created a negative image for the Okija community and would likely make its indigenes to turn a new leaf. The police have expressed their determination to expedite action on their investigation so as to enable them charge the matter to court.

Annex 3: Husband accuses wife of using charm to marry him

ON DECEMBER 6, 2012·IN NEWS   VANGUARD

Lagos – A civil servant, Adeyemi Jolugbo, 32, on Wednesday urged an Igando Customary Court in Lagos to dissolve his four-year-old marriage which he claimed he was forced into by the wife with a charm.

Jolugbo told the court that he had come back to his senses and was not willing to continue in such a marriage.

He said that his wife Bukola, was fetish and was not prepared to abandon fetish acts.

The petitioner said that Bukola, 31, took him to a cleric shortly after they met in 2008, for some incantations aimed at luring him into the union.

"When we got there, the cleric brought out two wooden dolls – male and female.

"He recited some incantations and asked me to say that I will love Bukola, marry her and listen to her forever. As I was saying this, he was tying the two dolls together with a rope.

"After that he told me to go and throw the two dolls in a river," he said.

Jolugbo said that since Bukola moved into his house two months into their courtship, he had been giving her anything she requested for, including his ATM cards for withdrawal of huge amounts of money.

"If I ask her what she used the money for she will not give me a satisfactory answer.

"When I was seriously ill, my wife did not take care of me; anytime she came to the hospital it was for my ATM cards."

The petitioner also accused his wife of regularly coming to his office to abuse him and tell his boss that he was irresponsible.

(NAN)